Crystal are you there? Luv G'ma

A sometimes shocking e-mail exchange between two age cultures.

Janet Arthur
and
Crystal Dent

iUniverse, Inc.
Bloomington

Crystal are you there? Luv G'ma
A sometimes shocking e-mail exchange
between two age cultures.

iUniverse books may be ordered through booksellers or by contacting:

iUniverse
1663 Liberty Drive
Bloomington, IN 47403
www.iuniverse.com
1-800-Authors (1-800-288-4677)

ISBN: 978-1-4502-6804-2 (sc)
ISBN: 978-1-4502-6805-9 (ebk)

Printed in the United States of America

iUniverse rev. date: 12/20/2011

Contents

Foreword

I remember taking care of my granddaughter, little blonde, curly haired Crystal, when she was about three years old while her mother, my daughter Emily, was working at a daycare facility. We were going to the library, and on the way, we would pass her mother's place of work. "Would you like to stop and say hi to Mom?"" I asked.

"No," she sweetly replied.

As we actually passed the building, I thought that she might reconsider and again asked, "Would you like to stop and see Mom?"

This time the response was a little louder but still, "No."

After we went to the library, on the way home, of course we again passed the building Crystal's mother was in. I hesitated but thought, *she's only three; why should I be embarrassed?* And so I could not stop myself from again saying, "Look, there is where Mom works! Do you want to stop and see her?"

She turned to me in her little pink, car seat and screamed, "NO!"

What was there about no that I didn't understand?

###

Fourteen years later, Crystal still seemed to feel misunderstood, and her normal speech was coming at us at that pitch. Since Emily and her children have always lived fairly close to my husband and me, we have been able to help them financially and emotionally through two divorces. Now, with her third marriage, and living even closer to us, it has given me a chance to witness the tension in my newly remarried daughter's home.

Of course, my immediate concern was for Emily and her happiness. But her decisions also affected her two children. They've had to move to a new house, change schools, and accept a new lifestyle with a new stepfather and a stepbrother. Yes, I could see the tension building.

Crystal believed her mother's remarriage was an incredible act of bad judgment. She felt that Emily was thinking only of herself and her own life.

However, I felt that Emily was hoping to provide a more stable family life by finally finding happiness with her new husband, Rick, a man who *wanted* to be her helpmate. She also felt very good about her new stepson, Justin, only seven and very appreciative and loving, unlike her own two, (currently critical teens). To me, Emily seemed to feel more at peace and secure than I had seen her in years.

But those same years had not been so kind to Crystal, a child that has always marched to her own tune. Between the ages of three and five she did what she now calls, "acting out"; her "acting out" consisted of getting down on the floor and pretending to be an animal, usually a cat or dog. Actually, she could usually get other children to play her game too, at least until they tired of it. I guess I saw this activity as leadership, but later I found myself wondering if it was creative or just a way to get away from her world.

As a small child, Crystal seemed to feel Emily's pain in her first marriage, and so the little girl was fiercely devoted to her mother and very critical of her father. Emily would always tell Crystal that she was going to grow up to be just like her.

Our daughter Emily is sweet and religious in character and tiny in physical appearance. She was a cheerleader in high school and graduated cum laude from college.

Crystal, on the other hand—although blond, pretty, and smart—turned out to have more of her father's genes in both personality and build. I don't know if that had anything to do with her changing behavior, but as she went into her teens, she obviously began to want to be nothing like her mother. Crystal became sullen and withdrawn, totally uncommunicative.

During her mother's divorce proceedings, I went far out of my way to pick Crystal up from high school. Daily, I would try to carry on some kind of conversation. Finally in desperation, my heated words to this silent teen were, "Say something to me tomorrow, or I'm not going to pick you up from school; I'm not your chauffeur, you know!"

But she said nothing; I guess that the words just hadn't formed yet. I was increasingly disappointed by my inability to draw her out or at least get her to be civil and appreciative of what our whole family was doing for her. My husband and I, her sisters and brother all came to Emily's aid. We ended up with a house for them, a job for Emily, and the finishing and selling of the completely unfinished house that the divorce had left to her.

By the time of her high school graduation, Crystal had a boyfriend, Trey, and that did help to give her someone to confide in; but it wasn't enough. And, with Emily's remarriage, sparks began to fly. I could see at Crystal's graduation party that she and her mother were increasingly at odds over Emily's new husband Rick. This got me thinking, so a few weeks later, I made a suggestion, "Crystal, why don't you start e-mailing me?" I thought that perhaps Crystal could use me as a sounding board to voice her unhappy feelings instead of butting heads with her mother. Once we began, I was surprised at the intensity—and the depth—of her feelings; she had finally found the words.

I know that my daughter wanted and needed to have some peace in her life, but Crystal and her brother voiced the same complaints to me—that their needs weren't being met. Nobody had asked their opinion about this new man in their lives or where they would live; to them, their lives were out of control. At this point, Crystal began constantly arguing with Emily and refusing to go to church, proclaiming that she was an atheist. In addition, she refused to even acknowledge her mother when Emily called for help with something. At one point, Crystal said to me, "If I wait long enough, she gets tired and does the job herself."

In the following e-mails, far from being silent and sullen, Crystal doesn't hold anything back. She rails against everything and anyone that offends her: her mother, the new husband, employers, teachers, Catholicism, etc. On occasion, she will ask my opinion about what she should do or say to protect herself from those that she feels have wronged her. The biggest surprise was that she could so easily articulate her thoughts and support them with both facts and experiences, since she had previously been so unresponsive.

In a few months, Crystal, at her mother's insistence, would choose to go and live with her natural father and attend junior college. You will read that we discuss religion, sex, divorce, family turmoil, politics, paganism, pedophilia, homophobia, and her personal social dramas. Crystal opens up before me, voicing her frustrations and views about life.

What I wanted to do was give her a safe place to vent her feelings and offer enough of an alternative view to give her hope for mutual family understanding of both our worlds.

Introduction

In the following e-mails I have listened and learned that Crystal is her own person and will do as she feels that she must. Her current cause is the gay–straight alliance, and she is marching to their tune. Personally, I think that that was just the bus that pulled up and that she got on. But she has made quite an impact with her speaking abilities on the subject and her mother is bragging about her leadership qualities. I do understand that she is now testing out her own sexual preference.

However, what I wish for her future is excellence in university and profession. I hope that she will be able to share her insights with teens who are going through the same emotional turmoil that she did. I would like a happy marriage for her (with at least one child) and good friends that she can turn to in times of trouble. Since she feels that she has not experienced a happy home life, I hope that she is intelligent enough to fill her own cup, so to speak. The experience of having a child changes you for life, and I wouldn't like her to miss out on that experience As I always say, "Life only presents you with so many 'golden rings', and I want her to grab onto as many of them (opportunities) as she can.

I am proud of her and her ability to stand up for her own ideas. I would, however hope that she will become able to give to her family a little of that compassion/empathy that she feels is so important in life.

In addition, I do hope that eventually she will return to the religion in which she was raised. It has been my observation that those who seek to change, only end up discussing it for the rest of their lives. It has always been my feeling that you should grow where you are planted, and then move on. Be the best you that you can be, don't try to change the whole tree of your life, just trim out the weak spots.

I hope that my exchanges with Crystal have at least given her as much to think about as she has given to me. Although, in the end I think that she knew my opinions before I gave them.

—Janet Arthur

June

This is the very first e-mail that Crystal chose to send to me. I suppose that she was trying to shock my Christian sensibilities—we have always been a very religious family.

June 23 from Crystal
Specifically look at proofs #7, 5, and 4.

I just stumbled into this website; it explains why God is imaginary. It's very well written/thought out. I'm rather impressed with this person's intellect and ability to put into words exactly why I'm an atheist.

Crystal

June 23 from Janet Arthur
Hi:

I went to the website and read proofs four, five and seven as you requested ... These are my opinions:

Proof #4: Think about Science

The article presumes that because events fall in a pattern, only man could have made this pattern. Indeed, the article states that, "Only by assuming that God is "imaginary" and prayer is "meaningless" can science proceed."

However, in my experience, science is on the side of religion. I used to listen to a minister on TV who listed just about every known scientist and all believed in God. To me, there is no other logical explanation than God created the world. And *He* did it using whatever format *He* deemed correct.

Proof #5: Read the Bible

In this part of the article, the author seems only to look at the Old Testament. For example, there is a lot of fire and brimstone in those pages. They were harsh times, and perhaps it took harsh rules to keep the people healthy and bonded together. Look at Moses, as soon as he goes up the mountain to pray, the people fall back into paganism and unhealthy action. (Exodus 33:19) We who live in today's world, may have difficulty in equating with those times.

The author goes on to say that if you actually read the Bible, you will find it leaves us "dumbfounded by all of the nonsense and backwardness it contains."

But, I say that when Jesus comes in the New Testament, the Old Testament is completed, his life is shown as an act of love, and we are asked to follow Him in His example.

I do believe that God is a loving Father who allows/ does what is right for us/the world, whether we understand it or not.

I have always been taught that the Bible is both revelation and inspiration: Revelation is a truth that comes from God. While inspiration refers to the thoughts sent from God to those who wrote the Gospels.

In life, we are given free choice—thus God allows us to choose the actions we wish to follow. He only gives us the guidelines to be one with Him for eternity. As Christians, we believe in the Bible—*yes*, this is faith.

Proof #7: Understanding Religious Delusion

In part of this website, the author compares the belief in Santa Claus with beliefs of organized religion. He compares the Mormon religion and the Christian religion and the Muslim religion, saying all are foolish delusions. The writer assumes that everyone who does not have a religious persuasion feels that those who do are silly and perhaps even nutty.

However, I would say that God comes to all races in a way that their cultures can accept.

As to Santa, a real Santa never lived. But there was a kind man in Greece, eventually called St. Nicholas, and from his goodness, I believe, this charming story of Santa emerged. There is also a story from the 1820s that tells of a traveler who would give out candy and cookies to good children, and he was called Kris Kringle. I don't think that these stories do any harm, and they do bring families together and joy to little children.

The article goes on to say that there is no physical proof that Jesus ever lived. However, the life of Jesus and the bible are documented in history—from written Roman history, to the fairly recent discovery of the Dead Sea Scrolls, as well as the oral histories that makes up a great deal of the Bible. After his crucifixion, Jesus was also seen by many of the people of His time—I suppose you can easily say that the stories of Jesus could come from self-delusion or mob hypnosis, but I believe that the events in the NT happened as recorded and for a reason.[1]

Crystal, I do firmly believe that, in life, nothing is random. Whether we understand the reason or not, God has a purpose; *He* is not imaginary.

Much Luv,

G'ma

June 27 from Crystal

The statement about Santa was to make a point. Of course, a rational person would not believe in Santa Claus, but a believer in Santa would still be able to answer every question with a response that makes sense to THEM. The Muslim faith, the Mormon faith, and the Christian faith—they are all equally ridiculous; the author's point is that believing in them is just as irrational as believing in Santa Claus.

And how is "God" a logical explanation of the world? "How did the universe come to be, Mommy? Is it "Magic?"

No.

There is a perfectly logical explanation for how it came to be, whether that is the Big Bang Theory or another reason, undiscovered as of yet. Just because we don't yet know how we came to be doesn't mean we should assume that it happened by magic.

Speaking of the Old Testament, one thing that really annoys me about it is that it says homosexuality is wrong; it says so in the book of Leviticus (32:19). Of course, religious people refer to it as though it is god's word and

---

1   From I Believe Jesus Christ is The Son Of God by Wayne Greeson: "Under the law of Moses two or three witnesses established the truth of a matter (cf.Deut. 10:15; John 8; 17; 2 Cor. 13:15; 1 Tim. 5:19)".

still relevant; fact is, that's the ONLY part of Leviticus that religious people think still applies to today.

Crystal

June 28 from Janet Arthur

Hi: Glad that you responded. I was thinking of you last night and hoped that you didn't think that I wasn't giving credence to your opinions. You know I love a friendly exchange, but not just to drag someone over to my side of the line.

However, your response interests me. It does make me wonder, though, exactly what value do you give to life? Do you think it is a meaningless existence that we happen to go through? If there is no "master plan," then what is there?

I can tell you that evil and good do exist.

I have made it my personal plan to surround myself with good people.

I am afraid of evil—especially—the evil that masquerades as a "good." There are so many things in life that are tricks.

The cashier gave me too much change, or I hit a parked car and no one saw me. I forgot that I had a lipstick in my hand when I checked out, and now I'm in the car; why go back? The next step may be that I really think that that sweater is overpriced; I'll just take off the tag and wear it under my coat. And these are minor transgressions, just wait for the really big ones, because the really big ones are built on the minor ones. I just "happened" to get pregnant—guess I'll get rid of "it."

Organized religion lays out a pattern for life that keeps us on a path of righteousness to which I do subscribe. In the OT, the rules were given to ensure the continuity of the tribe. Sex was to provide healthy, new life, not pleasure. Another example: "brothers don't sleep with their sisters; fathers don't sleep with their children," etc. There were also dietary rules for keeping food that was safe to eat on the long journey from Egypt (Leviticus 11 and Deuteronomy 14). To my mind, those were rules that had to be made at that time, for the good and the health of the community.

Do I believe that above all there is a loving God?

Of course!

We are finite creatures with finite capabilities. We create a fine network of life with our families, our choices, the people that we know and influence and those that we don't know by our example. I've heard you say that you think that there should be a "central, moral good." Where do you think that comes from? It could only come from the gifts that we were given. And I believe that these gifts were given by God.

Love, Grandma

June 28 from Crystal

I give very little value to life, actually. And no, I don't think it's a meaningless existence. Just because being dead means being dead doesn't make life meaningless. You're supposed to try to make life better for those around you and those who will follow you. And, of course, you're supposed to enjoy your life to the fullest. That is the meaning of life.

And those are the ultimate morals. Unless you were brought up under very bad conditions, or you've gone through an experience that has changed you for the worse, then you will agree that that is the ultimate goal. You don't need religion to believe or feel that. You don't need a god telling you that. You love your family and your friends, and unless you have a certain personality, that love will generally extend to other unknown humans on the planet as well. That's just the nature of a human being. That's the best nature of a human being. Again, you don't need a god in order to love your family and friends and others. But loving all those people will fulfill the ultimate goal and make the world a better place.

I don't believe that good and evil exist. Not completely, in one person. Good and evil are just perceptions and/or concepts. And the idea of good and evil varies from person to person. For instance, many people think that murder is wrong. However, I believe that murder is good as long as it helps to make the world a better place. Killing an insane serial killer would make the world a better place.

Following that logic, abortions also make the world a better place. Some people are not meant to have children. Some people are not meant to have children yet. A teenaged girl cannot provide for a child. A person who will abuse their child should not have one. Stupid people should all be made sterile.

Over time, values are subject to change, having a religious leader reminding you every week about the values that you've always subscribed to should generally keep your values in place. Now, that is why people need religion.

However, in my case, I most certainly do not believe in a god any more than I believe in Santa Claus.

Of all the belief systems out there, my favorite one is the set of New Age beliefs. As the Wiccans say, "An' do as you will." The New Age people are all about "positive change" and love and all that fuzzy stuff.

I love them to death, and I think that they are the most moral people of all. They do not base their morals off of a bible or anything like that. They could never ever justify hate, as the Christians easily can.

My therapist is my monthly moral compass. We don't believe in the same things, but, as I said, all that fuzzy stuff is what is right.

Crystal

June 28 from Jean Arthur

Hi: Again, this response that you "give very little value to life" interests me. You don't matter; I don't matter? If we were not here, the world would still rotate on its axis? It's so defeatist; this reasoning says there is no purpose for any of us to exist. Why love? Why make the world a better place? The teenage girl may as well kill her child; why not?

I say that there is a price for everything—if you make the mistake, the sooner you pay the price the wiser you will be. If you "accidentally" get pregnant, why should an innocent child pay your price—adoption is the answer here.

When it comes to good and evil, there are so many things that cannot be ascribed to mere insanity. There are many people who don't have a conscience, though they were very loved by their parents. I have read that Jeffrey Dahmer for one came from a very loving family, yet killed for no reason. I believe that when a person allows his/ her mind to drift to "forbidden" places—stealing, extra marital affairs, murder, and pedophilia, for example—

this person can fixate on the forbidden thought until it seems perfectly right. It can start as a casual thought but soon the mind is enticed to think more, watch more, and engages more, until the person is so far off the right path that it is too dark to find a way home. Wrong begins to feel right, and right becomes, unfortunately, wrong. We always have a choice; we can choose not to engage in these thoughts and actions or seek help to stop them. Obviously, I am not talking about the really mentally ill.

Prayer is often a good way to find your way back on track. The door to God is always in front of you, but the handle is only on your side. It's your free choice (another gift). I am reminded of a phrase that says "the greatest trick the devil ever played was to convince humans that he doesn't exist."

Actually, as far as murder goes, this is mostly political not religious. If the Wiccans believe in being able to do anything just as long as it doesn't hurt anybody else, then they and their desires are only protected by the laws of a Judeo/Christian-based government.

Luv,
G'ma

June 30 from Crystal
How can I say that I don't value life, but at the same time say that bettering the lives of others is the ultimate goal? I'll attempt to explain.

I do not value life for Life's sake. For example, the fact that an unborn baby is alive really makes no difference to me. A tree is alive, but someone had to cut some down to build my house. A cow is alive, but it had to be slaughtered so I could have my tasty cheeseburger. That unborn baby is alive, but it would be best to kill it now before it has to endure a hard life of poverty, where its mother is on drugs, and her boyfriends will molest it, and it will grow up to perhaps be a criminal, and not only will it contribute to the pain in the world, it will also use up resources that are not exactly limitless, thus creating more pain for more people, simply by existing. That's just one example.

No, I do not value life, but I do not support cruelty. It's called "Empathy", something most of us humans have. I don't need a god to tell me to help the meek, when all I have to do is observe and, therefore, pity someone in need in order to move me to help them. Empathy is the reason why I don't need promises of a great reward to motivate me to help and improve the lives of others.

I never said the two of us don't matter. Just because we're not going to keep on living on another plane after we die doesn't mean we don't matter now. I matter to the world, because when I see someone nearby who needs help and know I can help them, I do it. And when I graduate from college, I'm probably going to go into research or therapy, and help the world in that way as well. And in the meantime, I'm going to vote and follow politics and get involved in political processes that matter to me, and help the world in that way. Because of my positive impact on the world, I matter.

Just because I believe that when I die, I am totally and irrevocable gone, doesn't mean I'm a defeatist. As you can see by this whole email so far, I can be quite optimistic at times.

As for why we should make the world a better place, and why we should love … There is no reason. Perhaps, some are different and, it gives them the most pleasure to scramble over the backs of others to reach the top, they do their best to get rich and screw everyone else. But I don't believe that most people are that way

However, it is in human nature to love. And because we humans are aware of death and, therefore, fear it, it is perfectly natural to want to believe we are going to live forever, and it's perfectly natural to want to be immortalized in our actions, like by winning a Nobel Peace Prize. People want to be respected and loved, and so they would normally want to be immortalized in a noble act, which is why we all want to have a positive impact on the world.

Oh, and adoption is not the answer there. That child is dead, and so it pays no price. But if it lives, that child and many more people will pay a price. Overpopulation IS a very serious issue, plus it's normally not the SMART girls and boys who are getting pregnant in high school or in any other situation that would require an abortion. Why fill the world with more stupid people? The smart babies should have more of a right to life and resources than stupid babies. But the stupid babies would use up the resources, and make the world a worse place as well!

I also believe that there is absolutely nothing wrong with consensual, mutual love between two people of the same sex. Earlier you mentioned pedophilia, as if it compared to homosexuality, however, everything is wrong with raping a child. The child is scarred for life. But the gay couple may live together happily for the rest of their lives. And, by the way, happy people are much more likely to help a stranger out than an unhappy person. (This is a bit of common sense from my psychology textbook.)

The Wiccans Creed: "An' it harm none, do as you will." That is the only moral you need. A bunch of rules—like what the Christians have—only leads to loopholes. Gay people harm no one by being gay; therefore, there is nothing wrong with them and nothing "dark" about them. (Nothing is dark except for the whole angst, "I'm an outcast," sentiment, which is caused by heterosexuals such as yourself.)

As for what you said about the Wiccans …You are right. Going through life without harming anyone is only possible in an ideal world. The Creed is an ideal. We are many times faced with decisions where all outcomes are going to harm someone. And so, you are supposed to choose the option that will end up causing the least amount of harm.

Crystal

June 30 from Janet Arthur
Dear Crystal:

I am impressed with your writing abilities. Although I don't agree with most of your ideas and most of your conclusions, you present them very well, and I appreciate that you are sharing them with me.

Let me go back to your Santa Claus example: "What if those people "really" believe?" What you are talking about here is "faith." They don't see, yet they believe. That is what Christianity is about. Think about it. For example, if we prayed for a cure for cancer and our prayer was immediately answered, God would then become "our" puppet, and we would be in charge. Doubting Thomas had to see to believe, and Jesus said, "Blessed are they who do not see and still believe."

I believe that this is "life school"—that we are here to learn, and we stay here until we do. I believe that God is a just God and that he keeps giving us chances to learn the answers to our hardest questions, or to deal with our most difficult situations.

I have wanted to ask you this question: Just what, exactly, do you find so reprehensible about the idea of God? Is it, "I am the Captain of my Ship?" Or is it, "He never answers my prayers anyway?"

I believe that you were called, by name, from the beginning of time, and that God loves every hair on your head and has a very special vocation for you, if you just quietly listen to him.

Luv,

G'ma

June 30 from Crystal

☺ Thanks for the compliment! I'm surprised it turned out so well—I wrote it at midnight last night, and I kept forgetting what I wanted to say. I had to type the gist and then fill in the middle for fear of forgetting the end of the sentence!

Faith: People glorify that word; it bugs me. Why should I believe in something with no empirical evidence? I'm sure you've heard of 'Occam's Razor', right? The theory is that when there is more than one explanation for something, the correct explanation is usually the one that requires the least assumptions. Those who use science do their best to assume nothing. They're always striving to find the truth, unbiased. That is why when they say evolution is the best explanation we've got so far, I say, "Okay, then, I will assume that evolution is the right explanation until someone discovers otherwise." In the meantime, it really doesn't matter how exactly the universe came to be. It has no impact on any of my decisions.

Anyway, I really don't see why religious folk see faith as such a great thing. It's definitely not. Why should I believe in something with no evidence? Oh, because your god wants you to believe in it with no evidence? I think that is just a bit too convenient for your god. As for the answering of prayers, you say God answers prayers, and then you say he's not at our beck and call. Did you know the bible says that God has planned out our whole lives? So why would prayers make any difference? And as for the answering of prayers, I'm sure you pray for many things, yet the ones that come true, you undoubtedly say is a result of the prayer. But then when one doesn't come true, you say it's because it wasn't in God's plan, or God isn't at your beck and call. I hope you realize how that sounds.

Now you are saying that the meaning of life is to learn our lessons. Well, we all have issues. Our genetic code predisposes us for some issues, and the people in our lives also help give us some issues. Most of us are also quite painfully aware of what our issues are, or at least that we have them. We are, of course, quite focused on them— how we got them, how they've affected us, and how we might alleviate them or get rid of them altogether.

And, of course, it'll seem like we're always running into it. I'm going to bring my Psych textbook into the argument, again. When you are depressed, you are much more likely to remember times of your life that were bad rather than times that were good, and vice versa. And since we are so focused on our issues, it seems like we are always confronting them, until they are finally solved.

This does not mean that there is a god giving us the same problem over and over again until we solve it.

And as for your last question, "What do I find so reprehensible about God?"

But Grandma, I've already told you. I don't believe in a god any more than I believe in the Easter Bunny. I believe in science.

It's certainly not the whole "I am the captain of my ship" thing. In the end, we do what we do what we do. I'm not bothered by the fact that I'm tugged around on a leash by being the product of my genes and my environment. And, of course, in some situations you will have very little effect on anything. I'm not bothered by that.

As for "He never answers my prayers, anyway" ... Well, that's probably why many people are drawn away from the religious life. However, I already explained how I feel about prayer.

As for what drew ME away, in particular?

It was the homophobia.

I was like "Huh, that's not right, is it?"

And then I started questioning all of it, and I began to see what I see now. It may have helped that I was also in great angst at the time, because I was 14, but that was probably just coincidence. Teenagers are *angsty,* and they question everything they know in order to figure out who they are. That is the essence of being a teenager. And so it was with me.

Crystal

July

While I am having this amazing interchange with my granddaughter by e-mail, her mother is calling me practically every day in tears, telling me how disrespectful Crystal is to Rick and what a bad influence she is on her brother, Timothy. Emily feels that Crystal's anti-religious attitude and hostility are ruining their new life.

Emily is also beginning to experience some drastic health problems and cannot eat. At one point, she tells me that she wants Crystal to have a chance to be happy but feels that she will be unable to find happiness in their house.

For my own peace of mind, I'm still trying to understand where her strong anti-religious feelings are coming from. I know that Crystal is angry and wants more control in her life. When the marriage took place, it meant that another new man was coming into her house, and she couldn't stop it. I do believe that she tried prayer, and it didn't work for her—at one time in her childhood, she was quite religious.

July 1 from Janet Arthur
Hi:

I feel that so much time in life is wasted in rebelling at the way we were raised. It is so easy to blame your mother for any unhappiness in your life. Other lives can seem so much better than your own.

But I say accept your family and heritage, you are part of God's plan. To rebel against everything you were raised to be causes you and your parents great pain; be the best possible you God prepared you to be.

Aunt Amanda, for example, is very financially successful, and it pleases me that she keeps her priorities in order: she puts family first. Amanda took all of the upbringing she received in our home and improved upon it. Although holding vast responsibility, she never misses a game, a school activity, a meal with her family, or going to church, unless she is traveling.

A mother feels good when her child ascribes to the way she brought them up. It is an affirmation of her parenting.

When your child finally leaves your home, they have, as a priest friend once said, "the right to sit down on the curb outside your door and throw out all of the wisdom that you have tried to pack in their life suitcase"; that doesn't feel good. As a parent, you feel yourself to be a failure.

Faith: Actually, we spoke of this before—there is a great deal of empirical knowledge of Jesus: *His* place of birth, *His* mother's house, and the written records of those who personally witnessed his miracles. Now if you are talking about "God," then all you have to do is look around you. In this vast and endless Universe, millions of things had to generate perfectly for a man to develop. Could someone throw up all the parts of a watch, .i.e., gears, dials, face, etc., and expect to eventually see a watch come down? Uh, uh. Never in a million years.

The world is mathematically perfect, and that takes a mind more intelligent than we can imagine. Jesus "came down" and assumed the form of man. I imagine God as a loving father who keeps giving his children more and more chances when they cry and stomp their feet and say, "Nobody can tell me when to go to bed." But in the end, we have to go to "bed"—whenever and wherever God decides we do.

We understand that our knowledge is finite. We keep searching for answers to life's problems, medical problems, mathematical problems; we know that we do not have all of the answers to the things that bother our existence. Our brains even have difficulty getting around the fact that there are no boundaries to space. Everything that we know has a boundary.

To say that all answers can be found in science is backward. What we are looking for are answers that were in place from the beginning of time. We were created by a mind so superior to ours that we can only speculate and worship.

You tell me that the idea of God is not reprehensible to you. Instead you say, "I just don't believe." This is not an answer. I would like to know why you don't believe. Is it because you feel that your intelligence is far superior to the majority of the world? Every culture on earth believes in God in some form or other. American Indians with no European influence believed in a Great Spirit, a

Grandfather. Buddhists, Muslims, etc, all believe in God. It seems to be built into our genetic make-up.

If a majority of the people in this world come to maturity believing that there must be an intelligence greater than our own, that there must be a "Creator" of this very complex, complicated, and mathematically correct universe, then we, as a people, are acknowledging that there is God.

Human Sexuality: It is my opinion that many professed homosexuals feel same sex is "safer," less threatening to their way of life. However, their way should not interfere with my life or mores. Marriage, according to *Webster,* is a close and intimate relationship between a husband and wife. One can choose to marry the opposite sex or one can remain celibate as do "most" Catholic priests. The sacrament of marriage protects families and our way of life. Not everything that we "feel" like doing is always proper.

I do not fear homosexuals. I just fear the loss of my way of life. I feel it is threatened because of their demand for calling same-sex marriage the same name as opposite-sex marriage. To me it is not the same; the commitment between members of the same sex should be called, something like, a *contract*. The change to my way of life would come because I think that the home-life of children in a same-sex marriage would be utterly different than one with a mom and a dad; eventually, this could be societal altering.

Prayer: prayer is just talking to God—it doesn't have to have a special format. It is acknowledging that a power source greater that my own is listening, understanding, and caring.

Now, whoa, whoa, whoa to you, didn't I read in your e-mail that "stupid people should not have children?" Did you know that Oprah was conceived under a tree with a man her mother just chanced to meet? We don't have the intelligence to decide who stays and who goes. Many, like me, are late bloomers. Every baby aborted had a chance to become a genius and save the world. So there!!

Love,

G'ma

July 2 from Crystal

Grandma, you talk about homosexuality like it is a choice, but it is not. Being gay is just how you are. It's who you are attracted to. Have you ever personally been attracted to a woman? Anyway, they're finding physical evidence that it's something you're born with.

Oh, and if you think it's a choice, or just a path that they accidentally turn down, why do you hear so many stories about people who date the other gender like crazy in high school, going from one boy/girlfriend to the next, just to either hide the fact that they're gay, or to try to turn themselves straight? That's a pretty common story, you know. And anyway, there's really no reason to want to be gay in the first place, unless you ENJOY being ostracized. There's a shirt you can get online that says, "I'm just PRETENDING to be gay for all the social benefits it brings."

Then you speak of empirical evidence that Jesus existed: sure, there's evidence of that. As for the miracles, though, I don't think there's anything other than the records of witnesses.

"In this vast and endless Universe, millions of things had to generate perfectly for a man to develop." Sure, but it's all just chance. After all, what are the chances that everything would go just so in my life so far, and your life so far, and the world so far, so that we would be using these exact words and having this exact argument about these particular topics? What are the chances of this happening? To me they are very small, and yet, look, it has happened exactly this way. Bizarre things happen all the time. And anyway, that is why we haven't discovered any sentient life on the other planets in our solar system. It's because their conditions are not good enough to support teeming life, like our planet is. And it's pure chance.

In the words of someone else, it's wrong to say that I don't believe. It is better to say that I am convinced otherwise. Saying "I don't believe in god" makes it sound like there is a god and I don't choose to believe in him. Saying that I am convinced that there is no god is a much stronger statement.

And actually, you've hit it right on the nose. Of course, I think I'm smarter than the majority of the world for not still thinking that there is a god. However, it's not always about intelligence; many people are just emotionally incapable of being an atheist. People are afraid of death, and they want to believe they are going to live forever. People think the world is a terrible place, sometimes a hell, so they need to believe in heaven, which is physically impossible anyway. People feel lonely, so they need a god who can be with them at all times. People need to believe that people who do bad things will be punished by god, by the universe, by whatever, so that even if they escape the law, they've still got it coming to them. Of course,

21

people all around the world believe in gods, and of course they always have. This is why people often find religion late in life. They're afraid of death.

I, however, do not need religion to make me feel comfortable, and I have the intelligence to know that god is make-believe, and so I am an atheist. That is the story behind my non-belief.

Homophobia: You're views are based on your religion. That's why the only argument you have is a quote from *Webster's Dictionary* and the sentence, "Because … it's just wrong, okay?" I would like to know how it is wrong; how it affects the American family in any way.

And how crazy of you to say that a person should either have sex with the opposite sex or have none at all. That's just ridiculous—most people are incapable of that. Isn't that why the Catholic Church is running short on priests? Is it because they can't be girls, and they can't marry? And, doesn't it say in your bible that god ordered humans to have sex and multiply? It's in our genes to want sex—that's why it feels good. That's why we crave it. It would be unnatural to not want it or to deny it, just as it would be unnatural to stop eating or sleeping by choice, or to become a hermit. There is no reason to deny themselves a loving life partner and sex they can enjoy when it won't hurt anyone, just offend some religious people. Where is the harm and where is the threat?

Oh, and about your suggestion that some homosexuals see the same sex as less threatening, and that's why they're attracted to the life style. It's actually the exact opposite. We all know the typical story of the teenage boy who is too scared to talk to girls, especially the one girl who he's been ogling all year. Generally, it's the gender that makes you nervous that you're attracted to!

And you bring up pedophilia, which truly does do great amounts of harm. But that is not a sexual orientation; it is a fetish. Well, then, I present to you another fetish— S&M! (Sadomasochism) How do you feel about that fetish, just out of curiosity?

Love, Crystal

July 2 from Janet Arthur

I've been thinking that perhaps we have reached a stalemate on religion. I propose that we reverse roles and we conclude with me writing how you view religion and you writing on how you think that I view religion. We can see how close we come and discuss it. What do you think?

Luv,
G'ma

July 2 from Crystal

Oh that actually sounds like it'd be interesting and fun!

Shall I start?

"Religion is the most natural thing to have because there is a god, and he made us believe in him! This god is all-knowing and all-loving. All you have to do is ask for forgiveness for your sins, and he'll grant it to you. Pray everyday because you should have a good relationship with god and because prayer works."

How's that?

Crystal

July 3 from Janet Arthur

Hi: I like that—it's good and certainly simplistic.

Here's my take on your view:

"Religion is the anesthetic for the masses. It keeps us from seeing life as it really is. But some of us won't tread that same ol' path because we see through the fakery, and we don't trust those who do not. All the forming of earth was just pure 'chance.' There was an explosion or 'something,' and within the vast nothingness of space, matter formed.

"Over a millennium, plants grew of various natures that would eventually grow to feed the people that would somehow 'evolve' out of the dirt/sea. These people would, by chance, have opposing fingers and thumbs and be able to procreate. What they procreated would not matter and not become real until they appeared and drew a breath.

"Many ignorant cultures believed that when there was a storm or an eclipse it must have been caused by a superior creature that these people called God. And when crops failed or floods came, they would pray to this God to save them. Eventually order would return, and these fools would kneel down and thank this invisible God for answering their prayers.

"Some of these ignoramuses actually made up a fantasy about a man called the son of god and called him Jesus. For fun, they wrote stories about him and were willing to die so that these stories would be believed in the future. Those who did not believe were called pagans."

What do you think?

Luv, G'ma

July 6 from Crystal

"Are you kidding me? How could all this happen just because of an explosion?! It was quite OBVIOUSLY the work of an all-powerful, all-loving, all-knowing God!! Nothing happens by chance, and humans are far too complicated to be by chance. Why won't you see the light and come back to God? He loves you and wants you back! What, you think you're just smarter and superior to your parents and everyone else? Is that it? You're just being vain and rebellious. Like a kid. Ah, but you'll see the true path someday."

Hey, I didn't say that Jesus was a fantasy!! I just said he wasn't actually divine. And I'm sure they didn't write the bible "for fun." They probably wrote it because they liked what Jesus said, and they wanted to keep it immortalized. And, by the way, the Catholic higher-ups ripped the original bible apart and put it back together, so it would only contain what they liked and what also did not blatantly contradict itself

Oh. Did you hear my mom's kicking me out Monday?

Crystal

July 8 Janet Arthur wrote:

Hi: Actually, I was trying to assume your reasoning, not sniping at you. All you had to say would have been that I hadn't painted the right picture of your beliefs. I was waiting for you to send me a reasonable description of how you think that I feel. Sorry, again, if you thought that I was baiting you.

To summarize my feelings, I do think that God has great love for me and you. That when we die our *spirits*, that are the "best" parts of us, will remain and go to God. I miss my mother and father and do look forward to seeing them again. When I am gone, I will meet them at the gate and that is where I will wait for *you*.

As for your mother, I'm sorry that you are not getting along right now, but that's between the two of you. You know that I'm here looking forward to your "missives."

I think that we should each make up a list of new topics for consideration.

Love,
G'ma

July 9 from Crystal

I'm not mad, or offended, really. Your description was somewhat accurate. However, your true beliefs shone through in a very obvious way—by the way that you worded things.

As for meeting your parents at the gate—so you get to see them again, yeah? Then you get to spend time with them? And serve and worship God every hour of every day forever? That's what heaven is, yes? But it is also supposed to be eternal bliss … Now … how does that work, "eternal bliss"? Humans are wired so we can only feel happiness in brief spurts—then we must pursue the next thing. That's why people say money can't buy happiness—because you will always want more. That's how happiness works in the human body. But I suppose you'll just say that God is all-powerful, so poof! The nature of humans and happiness change when you're in heaven.

And how could anyone be happy worshipping someone? That's kind of weird.

Speaking of heaven, what do you think of this quote? "All demons were born and raised in heaven." It's not exact, but that's the gist of it. I just thought it was interesting when I read it.

Yeah, about my mom…Things are strained right now. Don't tell her I said this, but I know one of the reasons she kicked me out all of a sudden is because Rick is itching to paint my old room. He actually told me he wanted me out by the 4th of July so he could get started. He came into my room and was looking around and musing aloud about what colors he might use to paint it—right in front of me. And Justin (Rick's son) randomly told me that his dad said *he* might get my old room. It's obvious Rick was trying to get to me with all that. But quite honestly, I don't care anymore about him. I'm moved out, so he can't affect me anymore, can he?

Anyway, as for future topics: Why bother? We can just discuss whatever's on our minds at any given moment. Oh, but we haven't emailed about abortion yet.

Laters: Crystal

July 9 from Janet Arthur
Wow, there were a lot of "threads" in that last one!

Death: Do people fear death? No, I think that they fear the way that they will die (entirely different). How will I die? Will I end up drooling in some senior "home" facility? Will my children care for me? Will I have enough money to take me to the end of my life? Will it be painful? These are just some of the very real fears of death and dying. Dying itself should be a release from the cares of the world.

What to do in heaven anyway? I heard one story about a rich man who died and went to heaven. St. Peter led him down the streets passing many splendid homes, and the man thought, "Surely mine will be the best." Upon reaching his eternal home, he found it to be a small cottage. "Why so?" he demanded. St. Peter replied, "We only have the material that you send up to build with."

Cute story, but I think that heaven will be freedom from all infirmity, all pain. There will be no worry, no fear. There will be the sure knowledge of God's everlasting love. What could be better?

Hell, on the other hand would be the exact opposite, filled with fear and suffering. Probably the worst part would be in knowing that God had sent His own son to lead us to heaven, and using our free will, we refused to follow. God had given us all of the chances we needed to be with Him in heaven, and we decided to reject them and choose hell instead.

All demons etc.: It just sounds like some dissolute person's quip. Jesus also said, "Do not be deceived by the devil. Many will come in my name claiming, 'I am the Messiah,' and will deceive many who will end in hell." (Matthew 24:4, 5)

Too many "righteous" people think that they know the will of God and persecute in His name. But since the devil began as a fallen angel who couldn't accept God's laws, then I suppose that the devil would find great joy in leading a really good person astray to keep him company in his suffering.

Rick painting the room: Actually, he told me about it, and I told him how wrong he was. But I know that he sees your mother upset and wants to protect the woman he loves and just married. Also, let's face it, he has been at the receiving end of your scorn for a long time and probably wants to show that he has rights in the house too. I'm not defending him, just trying to see how he feels.

I told him, "Just wait until your son, Justin becomes a teen and ready to move out—it's a hard time for all of us, but the love is always there." Leaving the "nest," is not easy. There may be times when we, as parents don't like our children, but we always love them.

Abortion: I think it is a vile and inhuman act. We are not savages. You do the crime and you do the time as they say. Give that little person a chance to have what you have had. And you my dear have had a lot of love from many people.

Being away from your home: I know that you will miss Timothy, and he you, but going away is inevitable. Timothy has to make his jump from the nest fairly soon also. He needs to see how you react so that he can leave with respect for his parents and for himself.

My advice: Don't look back now when all of life is before you—make us proud of the way you comport yourself and of the ways you use your natural abilities. Be proud of who you are, because all of us stand on the shoulders of those who went before us.

My grandfather was a farmer, as was his father. My dad started on a farm and then went to work in an automobile factory, a product of the Industrial Revolution. He once said that he couldn't imagine another time as unique as his. When he was a boy on the farm, the radio seemed like "magic," and by the time that he died, Neil Armstrong had already walked on the moon!

Today we live quite privileged, educated lives, and I think that we owe our ancestors at least the same amount of hard work and drive that they put in for us. I feel that we are obligated to make our lives and the world a better place to live in for those who come after us.

Luv,
G'ma

July 12 from Crystal

I want to discuss masochism: someone once said the only way to explain to others why physical pain feels good is to compare it to crying, which is painful, but feels good at the same time. I'm reading an e-novel, and the main character is a MAJOR masochist.

Anyway, moving on … Do people fear death? Of course they do! Why else do people want to leave a permanent mark on the world? Because that's the only way they can immortalize themselves.

As for heaven: You say that people will hang out with each other all the time? Is that even possible, without a body? Furthermore, how is it possible to keep your memories if you can't take your brain along with you? After all, it would be six feet underground, un-stimulated, and rotting away. If the soul exists, and it has your memories stored on it, how is Alzheimer's possible?

Jesus said there are many mansions? Was that a word back then?

"All demons started in heaven" dissolute person's quip … Did you mean "disillusioned"? I like that quote because 1. I never thought of that before, though it's true. Demons are fallen angels. 2. Some serial killers are born to average, suburban families, aren't they? And there's also all the rich "emo"[2] kids and the wiggers.[3]

Rick told you about painting my room? You mean it was exactly as I described? He did all that to bug me? Sometimes, I think people believe I'm just being paranoid about him because I dislike him. I don't want to dislike him, but I just don't feel that he was the right choice for my mother; he is so controlling. And he is not my father!

About Timothy: You're right. I'm role modeling right now, aren't I? Mom has been so busy trying to get her life together that I feel I should stick up and protect him. I don't want Rick to influence Timothy, and so I tell him not to even talk to Rick.

I read *Many Lives, Many Masters* ☺ [like you suggested]. It is a little interesting, but it got redundant around page 100, so I stopped reading. Comments: 1. Freudians are weirdoes, because Freud was a weirdo. Still, their main assumption about how understanding your issues/roots help you to solve the issues is reasonable and works. However, this book is from the '80s, and I suppose this psychiatrist did not know that there are no memories before the age of three.

Crystal

---

2 "Emo" is slang for an overly emotional young person; heavy use of depressing adjectives. Society sees them as failures. Crystal says the "rich 'emo' kids" don't really qualify as real *emo's*, but they think they do.

3 "Wigger" is slang for a white male from the suburbs who tries to emulate African American hip.

July 14 from Janet Arthur

Crystal—Are you there? I just went through all of my messages looking for one from you. How are things at your fathers'? I know that you went there for the weekend. Hope all is well. Grandpa called Timothy and asked him to come over tonight and go golfing early tomorrow. I know that you worry about him.

Anyway, about abortion: there was an article that gave unborn children a voice; they were worried that they had become an endangered species and no one was listening to their screams from the womb.

I also would like to discuss parenting in general.

Mansions: I looked it up and some say it may mean "rooms."

Love,

G'ma

July 14 from Crystal

I didn't respond yet because I just got internet hooked up today.

As for that article … that's more than a little ridiculous. Unborn babies don't have consciousness and feelings any more than a tree does. Also, a person does not begin to form memories until around the age of 3, which makes me pity them even less, if possible. You can't compare them to people. They're just potential people.

July 16 from Janet Arthur

Hi—glad to hear from you. What makes you think that babies don't feel pain or have memory? I had a professor who had a friend with a child that remembered her whole birth and couldn't wait until she had speech to tell her mother. She said that she didn't like it when they cut the umbilical cord.

Also, logically speaking, a "potential" person isn't going to turn into a frog. That embryo has within it all that is necessary to grow into a fully developed person It has rights and status in the community. It can inherit; it can seek legal counsel (through a rep). I believe they say that a person sheds all of his cells every seven years, and we are all still developing. That doesn't make us more or less important. Thomas Jefferson thought very carefully when he wrote we are all entitled to "life, liberty, and the pursuit of happiness."

Luv

July 17 from Crystal

That's a very silly story (the umbilical cord). The kid made it up, or heard about how umbilical cords get cut, and made the comment. No one has declarative memories dating before the age of three. It's physically impossible. Your brain is not yet developed enough to handle it.

When I say "potential person," I mean they can either become a person or die before they do. And it has rights because the law says so. And its family loves it because it is part of the human essence to want your genetic code to survive and produce more.

July 17 from Janet Arthur

Hi—I certainly can't verify the child's story of remembering her birth, but I do know that babies feel pain. I have seen objective studies of that. The "old" brain that keeps us breathing and moving remembers everything.

When we were visiting the Grand Canyon, I fell down a set of stone stairs. This was long after the age of three, but to this day I have to have my hand on someone's shoulder when making any descent; my memory of the fall won't let me walk downstairs or just a slope outside, without support.

Also, a baby that is unwanted and unloved comes out fearful and unhappy—I can verify that with the "wisdom" of my experience.

But speaking of children, isn't it interesting that most people eagerly await the birth of their children; the very people who will replace them on this earth? God's plan is truly unique!

Luv, G'ma

July 18 from Crystal
About the baby now—Yes, it's true that your reptilian brain and limbic system is up and running. You can store implicit memories. Implicit memories are the ones that you are not really aware of—like knowing how to play chess is implicit and knowing your daughter's name is explicit. Babies can store implicit, but not explicit memories. And actually, now that I'm thinking about it, I think I was wrong about age three. Now I'm pretty sure it's age two. It makes more sense.

July 16 from Janet Arthur
Hi—Death and infant memory—don't believe everything you read in the psychology books—they give a perspective, and that is all. When Grandpa and I were in Magigorria (a religious village in Croatia), our group leader gave out colored plastic rosaries to people coming into church.

When she gave a yellow one to an Italian man, he began to cry. She was upset and asked why, and the interpreter told her that his son had planned the trip and died, so the father didn't want to come. But a Spiritualist told him that in Magigorria, he would receive a yellow rosary to remind him of his son and let him know all was well. It was then that I had the thought that there may be many planes of reality and that time and space are human limitations that only we are bound by.

I have had this interesting thought that our lives are so small, that the first Good Friday was just yesterday, and that we are given this little bit of time to learn our lessons and move on. We have all been named from the beginning of time and deserve our chance at eternity. To us, it seems like centuries, but I think that in God's time, it is just moments.

Immortality: I never thought of wanting to be immortal. I would just like to leave my grandchildren good memories of me like I have of my grandparents. Everyone thinks that they are unique—and to some extent they are—like snowflakes, but there really is "nothing new under the sun." We're born, we live, and we die.

The universe is mathematically correct and balanced. There is good and there is evil; if there is a front there is a back; we have a left brain and a right. We, for the most part, are a balanced people. Once in a while, there is a hiccup and we get unbalanced. Does God cause it or do we? I don't know, but I do find that life is much easier to live if I accept my small part and play it with all of the "gifts that I have been given" and don't complain that I didn't get more. You have many "gifts"; it remains to be seen what you will do with them.

Alzheimer's: The real you does not exist in your brain. When my mother died, I was there watching her—when her soul left, her looks changed. She looked like someone similar but not exactly. "She" was gone.

All demons start out in heaven. And, yes, I did mean a dissolute person, and what did you mean that you like that quote?

Rick: he really doesn't matter to you except to keep peace with your mom and family in general. We pick our friends not our families. If Emily is happy, then we all should be happy for her.

As for you—life didn't give you a "warm house," and so you have got to make that for yourself. Your mom loves you to the extent of her abilities, and if that left your cup half-empty, then you'll have to fill the rest yourself, and you have the gifts and understanding to do it.

Sorry, got a bit preachy there.

Are we going to talk about parenting?

Luv, G'ma

July 17 from Crystal

Psychology is science, not perspective. When the Psychology course I was taking taught me that those certain personal theories, such as Carl Jung's "collective consciousness," it was obvious, that he was referring to science. Of course, it also taught a lot about Freud—what he contributed to the field—even though, as it said, much of what Freud believed has been proven to be false. Still, he is an important figure in Psychology, and a little bit is still applicable—not to mention the stuff people still use today from him, such as "the Freudian slip," or "that person is anal," and the shoulder angel and devil (which represent the superego and the id, while the person is the ego).

But you see, you do want to be immortalized—preserved in our memories and preserved in heaven.

What do I mean, "I like the quote"? Didn't I say why? Because of how it applies to delinquent kids from the suburbs, and also I suppose because I'm an "angry atheist, anti-catholic bigot." Hmmm ... Is there a word for bigot that starts with an "A"? Then I could just call myself the Quadruple A!!! I'm kidding, by the way; mostly.

What do you mean my mom loves me to the best of her abilities? Has she been talking to you about how she feels about me?! What'd she say? And because you didn't deny that Rick did all that to get to me ... I'll take it as a yes.

Crystal

July 17 from Janet Arthur

Hi: I had a psychology professor who said that when a Psych. doctor is discussing, for example, a delusional person, he will just say, "He's crazy" (not using medical terminology). You can carry the science thing too far. Psychologists don't have the answers for everything—I believe that the human brain is the last medical frontier. Mostly, I think that the human mind is just too complex to figure out. So much of this particular "science" is just guess. But I do believe that anything that man can conceive of can be accomplished. I think it is in our "finite" wiring. I think that God gave us all of the cures for all of the illnesses, and we just have to stumble along until we figure them out.

Re: your mother: As far as talking about you, she has only said that she is glad that you and I are communicating. She looks forward to a time when she gets her "loving daughter" back. She longs for a close relationship with you, but she feels that the two of you are on such opposite sides of the street right now that you have nothing valuable to say to one another.

When you challenge her belief in God, she feels personally attacked. I don't share that attitude—to me the world is not black and white. I see many grays—I see your side and I see mine and I am not particularly bothered. I am telling you what I know of my daughter, not what she and I have discussed. Emily is a very loving, caring person and very easily hurt. You too love and care and are easily hurt; perhaps you are more like your mother than you think. However, she did repeat to me, that in desperation, she told you that you need to go where you are able to be the self that you want to be and that won't happen in her house. So it is very loving of her to let you go to your father's house and wait for the day that you can return to her in a loving way.

Love,

G'ma

July 17 from Crystal

Psychology: new, largely unexplored frontier of science!!! How exciting it will be to enter that field and do research!!

As for my mom: Yeah, it's sad that we don't get along. I think the distance will do us some good … Then, when our memories of bitter events have grown fuzzy, we will perhaps make amends.

I'm glad she kicked me out the way she did. I would have never gotten my shit together otherwise—I needed someone else to give me that finalized date to move out. I was dragging my feet. But anyway, yes, I think once the bitterness starts to fade, I'll learn some respect for her and who she is. I used to think she must be so dim-witted … However, she is amazing when it comes to schoolwork (she always gets top marks), she is a hard worker, and she's got that whole "motherly sacrifices" thing going on.

Still, I've hated her whole traditional housewife thing. One of the things I hated about going to church was the fact that even though it was my mom's car, Rick always drove. I do understand that he probably drives because it's a service he is doing for her—I don't really enjoy driving either. But at the same time, I can't help feeling like he's in the driver's seat because he's the man, and I hate it.

That's just the way she is. She needs someone to protect and take care of her. She doesn't want to be in the lead.

I know my mom thinks that I'm incredibly sexist because I am uncomfortable with men, and I know it's wrong, but I can't seem to change that.

I guess I just need to focus on the fact that she is who she is, and she's made a good life for herself. And regardless of whether or not I'd consider it a suitable life, it works for her and she enjoys it.

Still, she and I have shared bad history together for five years now. So it'll take a while for us to get over it and move on. And with the way we are … we may never move on.

Crystal

July 18 from Janet Arthur

Hi—

Re the Rick thing and the car: I bought and paid for my current car, but when we go out, I let Grandpa drive. Most men are incredibly sensitive about their "manhood," and as a wife, you don't want them to lose that; it makes them miserable to live with. On the other hand, when I started to work, it made me realize how hard it is to make a reasonable living. I marveled that Grandpa was so generous with his money. It makes him feel good to take me and the family out and be the provider. I can tell you that when I was working, I didn't feel that way. I had a hard time even tipping a waitress I would think, *"Nobody tips me!"* I can be generous with my time but not my money; I know how hard I have to work to work to get it. So there are opposite sides of the gender coin and it can be nice if, as a woman, you pay attention and appreciate it.

I'd be interested to know just what "bad history" you have had with Emily. What I have seen is mostly garden-variety teen rebellion. Emily just doesn't have the stomach for it. And by the way, you do know that your brain is still developing, and so you are making judgments based on your still narrow view.

It takes a long time to gain perspective on life and to learn not to make the same mistakes twice. To learn what is valuable and what is not worth fighting about. To learn that making an impression is valuable. It is the old, "give a teacher what she wants, get your A, and move on." Give Emily what she wants, it's no skin off your nose, and it's not pretending. It is just compromise—that's what you do with family, so that in the end the real love can shine through. Keep your eye on the prize! I love you both!

Luv, G'ma

July 23 from Crystal

Most men are sensitive about their manhood, eh? Well, I like to think they're building them a bit better, these days.

I'm not worried about anyone's "manhood" except for my own! Which is very sensitive, by the way, so please be careful with it.

The problems I have with my mom ... mostly it's that I do not respect her—which, I suppose, IS garden-variety teen rebellion. Of course, just because everyone goes through that same old "teenage phase," doesn't mean it should be disregarded. When you go through puberty, you begin to stop believing everything your parents and teachers and all other authority figures tell you, and you begin to have thoughts of your own. You start to figure out who you are, as an individual. Without teenage rebellion, everyone would have exactly the same thoughts as everyone else, and everyone would be very simple.

You say I should give my mom what she wants—well, let's see, what is it that she wants? She wants me to go to church and get along with Rick. And, I suppose, she would also like to have my love. Well, the first two will certainly not happen; because that WOULD be skin off my nose.

Now that I've moved out, I can call Rick an asshole to his face and walk away with no consequences. I've always been a very cautious person, and I've always had to tell myself "No, I can't do that, because then this and this might happen, and I don't want to deal with that on top of this." Well, now those days are over, and I love the feeling.

As for going to church: well, we both know that's never going to happen.

As for legalizing abortion, that would not give the government more say in our lives. Illegalizing would, though. Sticking a chip in your baby so you can track it—now that would be giving the government control.

Anyway, gotta go, bye!

Crystal

July 23 from Janet Arthur

Hi—Good to hear from you; I love our discussions. As to strong men, some things never change. Actually, I think that both men and women have suffered from the female revolution. Men used to know their place—they were to be strong, support their families, kind to females and the elderly, etc. Women got doors opened and respect from men for being the "weaker sex." Now we all know that that was wrong, but women are still running homes, having babies, grocery shopping, clothes shopping, and planning family functions, while many men seem to be confused about their role. They must think that if the woman wants to be strong, then let her go to work if she wants, let her open her own doors, let her carry her own weight. I know that I am over-simplifying, but there is truth in there somewhere. (No man could ever do all that women do).

Teen rebellion: It is a good thing; it helps to force the young'uns to want to go out on their own. Imagine— in the early West, a girl would get married, take some reminders of home, and never see her family again. It was too far and too hard to get there. Nowadays, the steps that you take may not be as far in distance, but perhaps they are even further in life choices. But in the end, compromise is the glue that holds a family together. Nobody gets their own way all of the time, so we have to pick our battles, and think about them carefully.

What do you get from listening to your mother or going to church with her when you are home? You get her love and admiration and understanding of your sacrifice. About Rick, I can only hope that she got it right this time. I love Emily and want her to be happy. If Rick makes her happy—fine. He has shown Grandpa and me a lot of compassion—not that I can be bought. When you are raised as I was, to be almost totally on my own, you learn to be very cautious about those that deserve your trust. As I have said before, I try to keep only "nice" people around me—I have a very suspicious nature. So don't think that I may be fooled easily.

Abortion: Legalized abortion would involve me. I want nothing to do with anyone's baby problems. I feel that this should be between the parents and the parent's doctor. If an abortion is necessary, then the funds for it should not come from my tax dollars. I don't pronounce judgment on those who chose death to life—I just want nothing to do with it.

By the way, I don't pronounce judgment on homosexuals either—I have just given you my point of view.

As you will find out, Crystal, life is so short. You just barely get enough time to get all of your learning in, and then its over. I read once of an elderly lady being interviewed on "old age," and she said something like, "It is like Saturday evening and the chores are done; all we have to do now is wait for Sunday to come—it's peaceful."

I don't know if I got it all in, but I know that you will tell me if I didn't ☺

Love,

G'ma

July 25 from Crystal

But women did not get respect for being the "weaker sex." They got told "you can't, you can't" over and over. That "you can't" mantra is only beginning to die off.

If things have changed for men then they will just have to find their new, proper niche and fill it. What do I think are some of a man's strengths? Well let's see … they can be stronger, and they can be funnier than women. And so what about women's strengths you ask? They can often be more serious, better at reading people, and better at academics.

But I think it's funny that some men may be confused about their "manly" role. As the "new weaker sex," they should simply do whatever their woman requires. Women can't handle it all alone, after all; we need some support at home. Am I joking or am I not? I'll let you decide, as it's more amusing that way.

Choosing our battles: I'm very well acquainted with that concept because I have to do it all the time with my dad, except that the battle never seemed to be worth the imagined consequence. Perhaps I will begin to forgo consequences soon. Speaking of which, I just remembered that at the Senior All Night Party, the psychic reading palms there told me to do just that. "Take a chance." Ha.

Regarding Legalized abortion: don't you think it would help the economy if the government did help pay for people's abortions? Legalization of abortion would make a smaller population, and all that; of course, some people would be bound to try to take advantage of it, I don't know. Still, legalizing abortion doesn't have to mean the government is investing money in it.

Crystal

July 26: from Janet Arthur
Re: the following website you sent me:

> Number of people God killed in the Bible = 2,238,344

> Number of people Satan killed in the Bible = 10

Hi—I don't think I get it. Is this the number of people that think that there is a devil? It says it is made up of bored office workers' opinions. Is it sarcasm?

I believe that God allows people the freedom of choice in this life and so some choose to succumb to evil. Therefore, I don't think Satan kills; it would be my opinion that he leads others to do evil. A long time ago, I read an article that said, as I recall, that the author didn't think that the devil would be so obvious as to wear red and carry a pitchfork—his feeling was that the devil would wear a three-piece suit, carry a briefcase, and be very handsome; we do seem to judge people by their looks

Earlier when we spoke wrote of moral obligations, you said that you considered voting important. What things/strengths do you think are important in elected officials?

Moving on to another topic, lets talk about your conflict with your mother—in her teens your mother wanted to be a gymnast. Even though I had four more children at home and tons of laundry to do, I remember sitting in gyms for whole days with your mom doing her routines—in Lansing or wherever—she was very good, and we did it until she didn't like the muscles that she was developing. I encouraged her to keep at it, because there was a possible scholarship in it for her/us. But most teens are alike—"You just don't understand, Mom!" No matter how we pleaded, she was all done and no amount of coaxing could change her mind. She was no different than you; she wasn't going to do something just because we said so.

But Emily has done well in life for herself, and we managed to pay her college tuition. Anyway, I must admit that in some respects I was living vicariously through my daughter. I was someone who couldn't even do a chin-up in gym class—it was a thrill to see my daughter walking a balance beam and doing a floor routine! But from my point of view, it would have been nice to get some scholarship money to help pay for her education.

Write soon, I always look forward to your messages
Luv,
G'ma

July 26 from Crystal

No, that's not what it was. It was a bar graph comparing, as recorded in the Bible, how many people God killed or had killed vs. how many people Satan killed or had killed.

As far as elected official's strengths: He/She should be: a great orator, with the ability to inspire others, and so to become a unifier for all of the people. And he/she should also have political experience.

Truth be told, I don't actually watch very much news (except the *Daily Show with Jon Stewart* and *the Colbert Report*), and so I don't know much about stuff that's going on. However, I don't think we should have a Republican president that is computer-illiterate. What we need right now is someone who can unify the country and *talk* to other countries to get them on our side as well.

As for the devil: the devil is not real. But if he was, then as the Tempter Incarnate, he would have to be a very attractive woman.

—Crystal

July 26 from Janet Arthur

I just read this article on abortion and wanted your opinion on a thought I hadn't had. It said that in Europe there are now more Muslims than Christians. Since Muslims obviously don't believe in abortion, (my opinion since Muslims have large families), they will eventually vote against abortion, and so, by their increasing numbers, change the European/Western world.

Luv, G'ma

July 26 from Crystal

Huh. That is rather interesting.

The obvious response to this is: Atheism cures over-population!!!

Crystal

July 26 from Janet Arthur

Back to the difference between men and women: Whether dating or married, we forget about the little things, the small gestures and compliments that make men feel like, well, men. And it is nice to feel protected. Someone once said, "We can still roar, but still, it's nice to do it through an opened door."

I do feel this is true. I already said that it was—and it still is—wrong to treat women as lesser humans. There was just a headline that declared that: "Oh My Gosh—girls are as smart as boys!"

Choosing battles: first, you have to decide if the relationship is valuable. If it is, then you can't criticize every action, and neither can they. That is where compromise comes in—you do it to keep the valuable relationship.

Abortion: Of course, I would end up paying for it. Where do you think these indigent women would get the money for an abortion? Many of them would use it for birth control. And doctors would get swept into this as well, if they could get free money for it many of them would go for the free money. We need to keep some semblance of civility for life to be worth the trouble. Suicide rates would probably go up as well.

One thing I didn't talk about is Timothy. I thought of that after I sent my last e-mail. You don't need to worry about him—you only need to take care of yourself. It's your time to be selfish—plan your future, decide what kind of life that you want for yourself, and get hoppin', *time's a'wastin'*.

Love,
G'ma

July 30 from Crystal

Okay, so basically what you're trying to get across is …
Some women need to feel like "women," and some men
need to feel like "men." Meaning … Some women need
to feel like graceful, beautiful royalty, and some men need
to feel like the strong soldiers protecting and providing for
the royalty. Isn't that right?

This is true. But I think it is becoming less common,
and I think that it is a good thing.

And I think it's kinda funny, "We still roar; but still,
it's nice to do it through an opened door." That strikes
me as hilarious, actually, as what you are really saying is
"Yeah, we're totally powerful and all that, but I still want
someone to open the door for me to roar through," Or …
"I'm independent and proud of it, but I still want someone
to treat me like a dependent."

Oh, but how can I not care what happens to Timothy?
He's *my* brother. MINE. MINE. MINE. So if Rick
mistreats him, it's a slap to *my* face.

And I know that I really should be selfish and just
focus on me, but … I can't help but give in whenever my
friends demand anything of me. I am certainly not ready
to settle down with someone—I haven't dated enough yet.
And now I'm off to college, and I know that I'm going
to run into all these sexy situations, and I'll be seriously
tempted to go after a few someone else's. But at the same
time, I'll have this boyfriend, Trey, who is utterly devoted
to me.

—Crystal

July 30 from Janet Arthur

What is it Aretha Franklin sings? RESPECT, really, that is what it is all about. I respect you for your needs, and you respect me for mine. I think that you are right that things are changing, so the rules adapt for the age. Grandpa, for example, is wounded if you treat him as though he is not able in any way. I respect that and try to be careful. A girl your age is living in a different age, but I'm not so sure that total Independence is necessary. Again, I will mention Kahlil Gibran and his poetry. He has a poem on marriage in which he says that you should be like two trees, neither standing in the shadow of the other (or words to that effect). And I like that—acknowledge me for who I am. However, sometimes women have painful periods or are giant with child—these are situations that men do not suffer—and we do mother their children, so I think that a little respect is nice.

As for your brother, Timothy: he is mine also, your mother's also—the whole family loves Timothy—perhaps not in the same way you do, but still we do. And it surely would be a slap in my face if he were mistreated in any way as well. However, he is fifteen now and does need to assume responsibility for himself. To be too protective is to cripple him—if treated as though he cannot care for himself, he will begin to believe that he can't do anything.

And speaking of your boyfriend, Trey: that is what selfish is all about. You cannot take care of old boyfriends like Trey all of his life any more that you can Timothy. If you are ready to move on, it will be a learning experience for both of you. Never let a relationship go on too long. We all need to have several relationships in the beginning, so that we know the type of people that are right for us when we do find them.

Love,
G'ma

August

Our e-mails seem to have stirred Crystal's desire to talk about her sex life but I don't think that she has been "active" as yet; she's just thinking about it.

To me it seems so rude to just come out and ask her about her sexual experiences—plus I am not sure if I want to know!

August 2 from Crystal
First thing I *have* to say (because it's still fresh on my mind) is that I had this really horrible dream last night in which I found out that I was pregnant. And in the dream, I was freaking out and thinking, "But I haven't done anything that could get me pregnant!" And "holy frick, I can't even get an abortion for another two weeks because I'm not old enough to legally do it yet!" And "Ah Shit, this is gonna be expensive!" Anyway, when I woke up and realized the dream was just a dream, I was so relieved. And then it got me thinking that though we have talked about abortion, we have not talked about abortion in relation to me.

As you've probably guessed, one of the reasons why the abortion issue is so important to me is because I would choose to abort if I happened to get pregnant. Now, I think we can both agree that I simply cannot have a baby right now, never mind that I never want to have one anyway. I'm 18 (almost), and I'm about to start college. If I did get pregnant and was forced to keep the baby, it would ruin my life, and I would probably come to despise the child. Forcing someone to keep a baby is like rape, except that the rape lasts for nine months and is much more physically painful for much longer. That's why one of the main things pro-choice people say is that it is a woman's choice, because it is her body. Anyway, I would definitely come to hate the kid, and we know that *that* is a bad environment for a kid to grow in.

Honestly, if I were forced to remain pregnant, I would most likely take a clothes hanger and perform a makeshift abortion on myself, then call my dad to take me to the hospital to fix what ever damage I ended up doing to myself. And I'm sure that if abortion became illegal again, many girls would take that route.

Anyway, as for respect: Yes, I completely agree—two people in a relationship must respect each other and understand that there are times when they should toe the line.

You're right about Timothy. He does need to take care of himself. I'm really worried about him because he *does* feel that he's completely incapable and a complete failure.

But anyway, yeah, ttyl,[4] as they say …

—Crystal

---

4 Talk to you later.

August 3 from Jean Arthur

Hi

Re your dream—I remember having a dream that I had a baby with dark hair and brown eyes, and I was freaking out I am fair and blue-eyed—I couldn't have a child with brown eyes! It really was a weird dream for me. Anyway, you keep mentioning pregnancy so the pregnant thought must be rattling around up there in your head.

The best way to avoid it, of course, is to promise yourself that you will avoid sex. Premarital sex is dramatized as completely normal and perhaps even necessary. Yes, you are a teen, and yes, your hormones are raging, and yes, abstinence is still best. Even more so, it is best that when you marry your spouse is a virgin too. It means that you both have saved yourself for the right one and you will share the "first time." It also means that neither of you will have a sexually transmitted disease.

We aren't meant to be consumed by just any casual passerby. It isn't easy to share your body with another person. If you let passion go far enough, saying no at the last minute won't work—you have to be aware of hurting yourself and hurting the significant other. As I have said before, everyone wants to feel unique, and once used and disposed of, you can lose that feeling—especially girls. For boys, it is often like a notch on their belt—as the old saying goes, "Why buy the cow if you can get the milk for free?" Sex for guys doesn't have the same meaning as it does for girls. For girls, it is a trusting and complete giving of them—it is not that way for men. They say (I think from MY Psych class) that a man thinks of sex every 3 minutes. Yikes!!

So abortion isn't really the issue, abstinence is. Becoming mature in this sometimes false, highly sophisticated world is difficult. But you're smart and have a good head for seeing through deceit. Watch for honor and decency in a man/boy—so often we are drawn to the "bad" boys, although I haven't seen that in you. But do give serious thought to the kind of man you would want to spend your life with. Would he want to have casual sex or would the "person" be important to him? Now we're back to RESPECT for ourselves and others. We don't just "give" ourselves away and expect that there will be no price to pay.

Of course, pregnancies do happen, and adoption is a wonderful thing. It is, of course, 9 months out of your life—everything has a price. But please, don't fixate on this; you are surrounded by people who love and care for you—you would never be alone. Just enjoy your relationship with Trey as long as it has meaning to you both. (Not *too* long though).

Hope I have said something of value.

Love,

G'ma

August 3 from Crystal

I've noticed that Mom is trying. She's been emailing me.

"Men think about sex every three minutes …" I thought about sex all the time maybe four or five months or a year ago. I miss it; it was great. Ever since then I feel like I've lost my mojo. But I try not to think about it, because when it comes to thought patterns like that, thinking will hurt, not help. I'm not ready to get sexually involved yet.

Funny story about me and sex—the other day, my dad said that I'm allowed to have sex with a feminine girl, but I can't have sex with a boy or a "butch."

"But Papa, why can I have sex with a girl? He said, "It's because you can't get pregnant that way".

"So then I asked, "Why can't I hook up with a butch"? He said, "Because butches like to use strap-ons"

Yeah, my dad's a funny guy.

I know that you are trying to warn me against premarital sex and I know that you mean well. Premarital sex has been depicted on TV as completely normal, and so it has become that way—in the real world. The relationship between society and TV is that society affects what's on TV, and TV affects the nature of society. Still, I'd guess that somewhere between a third and a half of high school seniors are virgins.

But anyway, I don't agree with you about premarital sex. I mean, do you know for a fact that it's better when a new husband and wife are both virgins?

I actually have met one guy who told me he was going to wait until marriage. Kevin Brewer, I had lunch with him. He was SO FUNNY. And by that, I mean I was amused by him, not that he was actually funny. I would talk about sex around him a lot, just to get his reaction. The kinkier the sex-talk got, the funnier the look on his face. Still, I did my hardest to get him out of his shell, but to no avail. Anyway, the poor guy was certainly not the most attractive—he was what you would picture a nerd to look like: pale skin, glasses, really short hair, and posture with his face-thrust-forward. Not a pretty picture.

So, most likely, he will succeed in that whole waiting-for-marriage thing. He's really not much of a catch. The closest he's ever been to a female was by dancing with one —he never had a girlfriend. Word on the street is that he asked one girl and she turned him down—and was very mean about it.

Anyway, what I'm really trying to say is that normal people these days don't wait, or if they say they're going to, then they find out differently when they finally do get serious with someone. I knew a girl who said, "Maybe that happens to other girls but not to me. I'll never change my mind about premarital sex!" Turned out that girl was wrong; she didn't wait.

Anyway, animals are programmed to pass on their genes—we are all drawn to sex. That is the way it is, and I believe television has only made it more acceptable, and simply somewhat more likely.

Now, of course I will have to disagree with you about the whole giving-yourself-to-someone scenario. I don't think girls think about it like that anymore.

Speaking of "makin' love"—that term seriously annoys the hell out of me, and I'm not entirely sure why ... but it makes me cringe every time I hear it or read it. I mean, the term doesn't even really make any sense! Are you really creating love with this person? Is having sex how you form affection between each other; because that seems a bit shallow to me. It just bugs me is all, like ... it seems like someone came up with the term so they wouldn't have to say "have sex," because that sounds dirty to them or something. I once had this conversation with Mom, and she replied that "having sex" didn't sound intimate or romantic to her—she said it sounded loveless.

No, I think it's the term "intercourse" that relays a lack of love. . Then there's "screwing" and "fucking," which are both dirty, naughty terms. Then there's "having sex" which to me sounds like … well, having sex could mean anything, and you'll know exactly what it means, and the level of affection if you know the couple that is doing it. Then there's making love, which to me is a very prudish word, and which I never, ever want to hear someone say, ever.

Abortion IS the issue, because the general populace will never consent to abstinence, as it is very unnatural. Birth control is the issue. We must find better methods of birth control—condoms, I think, are only like, 92% effective. There is one contraceptive I've heard about that gets put in place by a doctor, and it seems like it is perfect … Takes a few minutes for your gynecologist to put in; it's totally removable; it lasts for 5 years. No maintenance (except to make sure it's still perfectly in place), no discomfort, and no mood breaking, which condoms are pro's at doing (mood breaking, that is).

"Once used and disposed of, I will no longer feel unique," you say. The thing is, the way that you describe sex is not the way that I do. It means something different to me than it does to you. It's an intimate thing you do with someone you care deeply for and someone you lust strongly after. When the two of you care deeply about each other, and you want each other like crazy, that is what gives the sex its meaning. Just because it isn't your or their first time, doesn't mean it loses any meaning, or becomes any less special. And if that "novel experience" is what you need to make it special, fear not, everyone is different so sex with everyone is different.

And no one that I would ever have sex with would make me feel used and disposed of. Unless, of course, I was using them for the sex as well ... and then I still would not feel used and disposed of, because I or the both of us would be the user.

Oh, and "Why buy the cow if you can have the milk for free?" Well, because you love the cow and what to keep it forever, that's why! Are you saying that a man will marry a girl just so that he can have sex with her? Tsk, tsk, Grandma—that is both pessimistic and untrue! Or are you saying that a man needs the promise of sex in order to entice him towards marriage? That is still pessimistic and untrue.

About "bad boys"; yes, that is absolutely correct. I have never been attracted to the "bad boy." Quite frankly, I am mostly not attracted to boy's altogether. However, the rare few can catch my eye. Trey is one of those. He is cute, feminine, vulnerable, and sweet. That's what I'm really attracted to in a guy. Masculinity and muscle turn me off. Androgyny is great, and so is a friendly/comfortable air.

Anyway, write back, of course!

—Crystal

August 4 from Janet Arthur

Where do you find this stuff? Yesterday you sent me an e-mail titled "Silly Comic," and it's not silly to my mind. I get the religious message; people walking in the dark being told that there are dragons *out there*. Once the light is turned on we can see there are no dragons at all, it was a scare tactic to make us believe that God sees everything and will punish us if we don't follow His laws and believe in him. Therefore, God and His commandments don't exist. I see the sardonic humor, but why do you suppose it was necessary to use the word faggot to those who wanted to see? And why "fuck you"? I always think that the "f "word is what unintelligent people/writers use when they run out of ideas. I turn off any movie that uses it more than ten times—I do count—for Pete's sake, why waste my time on a no-skill script? THERE ARE GOOD WORDS OUT THERE!

Also, I am so sorry about what your father said to you—there are no words … and it's not funny! What a terrible thing to hear from your father.

Love, G'ma

August 5 from Crystal

I suppose the person who drew the comic thought the same way you do about those words, because the character that used them was Religion. Why was it necessary to say "faggot"? Because Religion tends to disdain homosexuality, I would guess

The F-word … When you see it on the streets, it does tend to mean unintelligence. You'll see middle school (and some high school) people use it all the time, every other word practically. Then there are people who use it when we're upset or angry, like me. Then there are people who just like to be offensive and derogatory, who will use phrases like "holy fuck!" And "fucking A!" or "holy cluster-fuck!" is sometimes used if they want to be amusing as well.

Movies (and comics, too) are a different thing, though, because in a story, the characters are who they are. If they are the type that is going to say "fuck" all the time, then that is that. For instance, if the movie is about mobsters or gangsters, you're going to hear "fuck" a whole lot. I'm not saying it's always the character that is apt to use the word, but blaming the writer for their characters' personalities and vocabularies isn't necessarily fair.

—Crystal

August 6 from Janet Arthur
Hi: I was just re-reading your e-mail and realized that I had not made it clear—and perhaps you know this—that the contraceptive that you describe does not protect against sexually transmitted disease, only pregnancy. And that would probably be the least of your possible problems.

Also, I heard a word used on TV that made me think—coarse—something that I hope that you would never be. I knew someone when I was a child, Nancy, who used to come over to our house and act like she felt we looked at her like she was from the circus. (This was before my mom died) My sister and I were so sheltered and "girly." We did think she was coarse—she acted like a truck driver—didn't use intelligent language, her dress was sloppy—she obviously didn't think well of herself, and somehow she knew we didn't either.

This is just to say that we tend to tell the whole world a lot about ourselves before we even open our mouths. And it only takes one meeting to form an opinion about a person—don't burn any bridges with your crunchy exterior. You were raised to be a fine and intelligent person—don't spit on it now. I realize that this is an experimental time for you—and I love you no matter what—but I do have high expectations for you when all of the anger gets out. We haven't seen the best of you yet. Please don't start school firing off these "rockets" of baiting others just to see their response. Watch and wait, try listening to the kindness in voices and seeing the goodness in others; be a true friend, one that they can rely on. Don't worry too much about the future; we are all here for you.

Love,
G'ma

August 5 from Crystal

Yes, I know that condoms are the only thing that can protect you from sexual disease. (And they're not exactly 100% on that …) But some prescriptions do prevent pregnancy at 99%, which is the best. So that's half of the risk of sex taken care of. If you and your partner both get tested, and you're both clean, then that takes care of the other half of the risk.

Coarse? Me? Naw! I mean, well, perhaps I am not always the most sympathetic or sensitive person, and perhaps I am a bit indecent at times, but coarse? Well, as you might have guessed from knowing how I am, stupid is probably the worst thing someone could possibly think of me. That's my worst fear, that when I'm with someone I don't know—I will come off as dumb.

Don't worry about me baiting people at school. I'm actually very quiet if I don't know anyone yet or am in an unfamiliar place. Still, I must admit that I do very much enjoy freaking out the prudes … and the Christians. 'Course, that'll probably wear off in a few years. Then I'll try just acting like a good role model—and not a scary one! Seriously though, don't worry, because I am very kind to everyone unless they offend me personally. Even then, I might cluster near them to chat them up just for amusement value! And that is what I did with Kevin Brewer Ha ha ha.

—Crystal

August 8 from Janet Arthur

Hi—. Again, regarding our views on homosexuality: to clarify, I might say that it is not only some "religious" people who distain homosexuality. It is just not average behavior as most people today view "average." I understand that no one wants to be called abnormal, but the truth is that homosexuality isn't the "norm." However, as more homosexual families are depicted on television and more prominent people "come out," I do see more acceptance of the lifestyle and perhaps it will become part of "the norm".

I also would agree with you about the F-word. Grandpa and I watched a movie last night, *The Departed*, and the word was used a lot and in context with the work. However, I would say that I often hear the word just thrown in—when it does not add to the character, it eventually becomes offensive to hear.

Love,
G'ma

August 8 from Crystal

Well, what's wrong with being abnormal? No one is completely normal. And gay people can be a quite normal without "the Normal Sexual Preference." When you hear the word "normal" thrown around in regards to homosexuality, I believe what they really mean is that gay people are people too, and it is completely normal to fall in love with someone. Know what I mean? Even if what they say is that it's normal to be gay, you know they just mean it's normal to have a preference and act on it, yeah?

Crystal

August 8 from Janet Arthur

Referring to an earlier e-mail, (August 2), why are you so focused on getting pregnant? If you move in groups that have casual sex, then there is no safe sex. At your age, if you started having sex now, by the time you were ready to settle down with your "true love," he might be one of the ones who "waited," and you would be too experienced for him.

Having a baby is not the worst thing that can happen, but it certainly would be inconvenient—so don't start the process. I believe that most "good" guys, like Trey, feel that they want to wait too. They are not ready to be fathers *or* lovers. They just want to experiment, and there is no use being the test tube.

Luv

August 9 from Crystal

Well, it's because the pregnancy thing bugs me.

"No use being the test tube"? Silly expression! Tee hee, it's a pun!

But anyway, you say test tube like it's one-sided, or something

Crystal

August 16 from Janet Arthur

Hey—it's Saturday morning, and I have searched for a new e-mail from you ☹ I'm getting nervous thinking about my upcoming knee surgery—I need diversion—pullecz send me some! ☺

Luv,

G'ma

August 16 from Crystal

Huh. I was waiting for email from you

August 17 from Crystal

I got a job!!!

It's at a Donut Shop, about 2 miles from the house, a 15-minute bike ride.

I had an interview this morning at 10 o'clock, and I was basically hired because I said "Yes, I can work weekends."

I'm really excited about this job, because I'll be working the same days every week, so if I want to make plans a month ahead, I can, knowing which days I will and will not be available. Also, I'll be working with donuts and coffee!! So, I'll leave work smelling good. The day I filled out the application to work there, I spent 5 hours riding around looking for work everywhere, including McDonalds and Wendy's and stuff. I was desperate, and they were rude. But now I'm really relieved.

You know what else is great about the job? (Other than going home smelling like delicious, baked goods as opposed to grease?) She said I can bring homework and do it there as long as I've got my work done!!! That's a nice perk.

Crystal

August 17 from Janet Arthur

Congratulations!! That is just great. And about the guy that was rude—just remember that when you are in the position of hiring/firing. Always be considerate of others, even if they are young/old or different in any way.

Proud of you,

Luv,

G'ma

August 18 from Janet Arthur

Back to our homosexuality topic: When I discovered that I had breast cancer, many years ago, I was very angry. I wasn't mad at God but I was angry with my body for "betraying" me, *that is what it felt like.* I suppose that some people might be mad at their circumstance and blame God for their pain. From what you say, many homosexuals are bullied and harassed by those around them, that can't be pleasant—this could also apply to anyone born with any crippling affliction that would cause them to be teased by their peers. As they say, "It isn't the hand that you are dealt; it's how you play the game." Accept things as they are or let life demolish you. Some years ago I had a complete mastectomy and reconstruction to both breasts and vowed never to look back on the decision. As it turned out I could have had a lumpectomy, (not so drastic), but chose not to. I have never questioned my decision, I just moved on with my life. But I do understand that I am, "physically" not completely "normal"; and I know that God loves me the way that I am.

I had a doctor once who said, "I see hundreds of patients, and none are perfect." We all have something a bit different about us, and we can accept that difference or let it drive us to emotional instability. As for me, I have my *Igor foot,* an inherited trait; toes on one foot that are not straight. As a teenager I was so embarrassed by it that I wouldn't wear sandals in the summer. How I hated that foot as a child and teen, but then when I went to a doctor to have it surgically repaired, he said, "Why, you can walk just fine, and you're not a movie star." I suppose that I could have insisted, but I had lost the desire and really didn't want to hop on crutches for something superficial. Another abnormality!

Your mother gave me a book, *The Shack by William Young*, which deals a lot with those aspects of thought. I am currently enjoying reading it. It makes you look at God and life in a different way.

I suppose that I should comment on the evil Bible thing that you just sent. It was a website that showed the slaughtering of the Midianites (Numbers 21–31) and the killing of non-virgin women. I'm not defending it, but I really don't get into the Old Testament much. I think that it is a record of uncivilized times, and I am glad that I was not a part of it—these times are hard enough for me! At the same time, as I have said before, I believe that we live our lives on the shoulders of those who have gone before us. Building a civilized society has taken so long and we still have ground warfare which I think is an anachronism. We sometimes follow the rules that were made for a different time; for example, the outlawing of homosexuality. There are still a lot of things in society that are unfair (race, color, shape and size prejudice etc.), we work slowly to change these injustices and to make the world a better place. I have always promised myself that I could never be the person who "ran with the rope." That is to say that I hope I could never follow mob or group mentality. I hope that I would always look for truth and justice and kindness. I am searching my mind here—I want no part of darkness, for if there is darkness then there is light. I choose the light. I believe that all light and good comes from God, whether or not I understand His reasons.

I hear you struggling to voice your anger at injustices, and I applaud your desire to do so. You are, at heart, a very tenderhearted individual, and the world needs more like you. The hard thing to accept is that—I wish I could quote the bible, but something like—it is easier to see the mote in another's eyes than it is to see the log in your own. That is to say that it is easier to judge another person's minor flaws than to see our own major ones. All we can do is to keep on trying to do the right thing.

Luv,
G'ma

August 18 from Crystal
You speak of the churches' non-Christian activities? But it was done by the church. The church represents Christianity. Just because Christianity has changed over the decades, doesn't mean what happened back then wasn't Christianity. As for the evil bible website I sent you, those were things from the bible, which is supposed to be the word of god. I was just wondering how the word of god fits in to your belief system.

Many gay people leave the church because it makes them out to be evil scum. They come to terms with their homosexuality, and then they realize that their church will never come to terms with their sexuality; they're frustrated with the treatment they get, and they start to question whether god exists in the first place. Then they realize there is no god. Just because the bad treatment they get is what gets them thinking about whether or not there is a god, doesn't mean they are forsaking their creator. It's just opened their eyes.

Crystal

August 18 from Janet Arthur
Hi—

Just to clarify—when I said earlier that there is darkness and there is light, I want to add that I choose the "light" freely—not because someone tells me to, but because that is where I feel best. I want to see goodness in the place that I have been planted. I want to feel secure in a loving God. That is not to say that a priest paying too much attention to my son or daughter would not raise a red flag for me.

I often think that I was too overprotective of my children. I did not like it if even a waitress made too much of a fuss over whoever was my baby at the time. I do think that you cannot be too careful, and that is why I worry about you. You know the difference between good and bad, and yet you are so tempted by irreverent thoughts. You seem to seek to find some kind of truth in negativity. Do be careful.

You know that I love you.

G'ma

August 19 from Crystal

People who "willingly choose" evil are either teenagers who do it to be cool, or psychopaths who are crazy. Every normal person on the planet feels that their beliefs are justified, believes in their own goodness, and all that. When people do evil, they find ways of justifying it to themselves. Or they feel that they are making up for the bad with all the good things that they do as well. That's human nature; you don't need god to feel the need to do good things

I do know the difference between good and bad, and no, I don't have any problem thinking irreverent thoughts.

Crystal

August 21 from Crystal

Grandma—

Timothy is having such a hard time now, and I don't know how to help him. His best friend just dropped dead at school while running track. Tim has just shut down. They found him hiding in his closet, and he had cut marks on his wrists.

I'm the only person who's thinking about him. My parents were only thinking of themselves.

I'm probably going to call Rick soon to chew him out for not being more understanding of my brother. I don't live there now; so I can do that. But what do you think?

Crystal

August 21 from Janet Arthur

Dear Crystal,

I know that you are worried about Timothy. The death of his friend has caused him terrible grief. I know that it must be very frustrating for you not being able to help him. I too am concerned about him. I fear that it is going to take a trained professional to help him through this rough patch.

It's not easy raising children and trying to give them the best life that you can. It hasn't been easy for your mother and I also know that it has not been easy for you or Timothy. At present neither of you likes Rick. But, as I have said before, if Rick makes Emily happy then good—it is up to both of you to go on with your lives and make the kind of solid family that you want. Really, you know in your heart that Emily has worked and sacrificed to give you the best life she could. It is easy to criticize someone, as the Indians say, "when you haven't walked a mile in their moccasins."

Love you,

G'ma

August 24 from Crystal

To Grandma—

Timothy says a counselor can't help him, because they don't know him and they're getting paid to listen to him. I told him that the whole reason psychologists go into the field is to help people, but if he really wants to be sure the person is genuine, he should go to a young, just-out-of-school counselor. I told him if he doesn't like the counselor he's going to, to tell Mom to find him a new one, but he says he's not gonna do that, because no counselor can help him, because no counselor can really get to know how he feels.

You still haven't told me what you think of me telling Rick off. I honestly don't know exactly what I would say.

—Crystal

August 25 from Janet Arthur

Dear Crystal—

I like that you encouraged Timothy to see and talk to a counselor, because he really needs professional guidance now. It is really good that both your parents understand the problem, how ever it came about. Timothy feels lost and confused, and obviously thinks that it's *his* body and he can do what he wants with it.

As far as calling Rick, I have already answered you on this subject—I can't get involved or give you advice on family matters that belong to my daughter. If I see something that is not right, I will do something. But your views and feelings are your own, and I can't act on them or even have an opinion, without causing more problems between Emily and Rick by my intervention.

As I keep saying, Rick makes Emily happy, and if he makes Timothy unhappy, then Rick will lose Emily. Believe me; mother-love is very powerful.

If you get into a fight with Rick, it could rebound on you and make Emily defend Rick and take the emphasis off doing the right thing for Timothy.

You have had a lot of adjustments to make, and so has Rick. He wants to do what is right, and when he sees you and Timothy hassle your mother, he wants to defend her. Remember, Rick never saw you when you were "cute and cuddly." He also wants his own child to have a fair share of the attention, and so he is very sensitive to any comments about his son.

You need to take yourself out of the equation—I know that it is hard because you see Timothy's side of everything, but that doesn't mean that you see the whole picture.

Timothy has many talents, and we all need to help him see that he has them. We all walk a narrow line of freedom. We really don't think that the State could enter our lives and make decisions about our family, but it can. Children who have emotional problems can be removed from a home. Timothy needs to feel loved and competent and cared for. You can help him turn away from his sad thoughts and feel that our family is behind him and loves him unconditionally.

Love you, sweet thing

G'ma

August 26 from Janet Arthur

It occurs to me that, in many instances, you can only have one person in charge. I know that you want to help Timothy, but reading aloud to him and helping with his homework may only add to his feelings of incompetence. In Timothy's case, it really is his mother and father who are responsible. Try to trust them, because it can only confuse Timothy to have you telling him one thing and them another.

I do believe that he needs you to be supportive, because he trusts your judgment; you can encourage him in the path that he chooses. This is an important role—but not the major one. His parents have sole right to that.

Should you choose to give yourself the enjoyment of your own child, you too will have to accept the good times with the bad.

Luv

August 27 from Crystal

Except that I don't believe in any of that—Timothy is a person, not someone's property. I do try to point him in the right direction, but he doesn't listen to me.

And no, you can't actually use this argument as incentive for having a kid.

Crystal

August 27 from Janet Arthur

Hey—you know what? I think that I received an e-mail from "someone" saying that "Timothy is mine, mine, and mine."

Anyway, no, I wouldn't use that small statement as encouragement for having a child. But it was interesting to me that, years ago, when asked to introduce myself to a neighborhood group, all I said was that I was the mother of five children—I had gone to college and had an interesting job, but I guess, deep down, I feel like mothering is the most important job that I have ever held thus far.

I suppose, because I love you, I would want you to have the same fulfilling life experience that I have had. Truly, mothering brings out a part of you that you never knew existed. It is one of those "golden rings" that life presents to you and I want you to grab them all. ☺

Luv

August 27 from Janet Arthur

Hi—it occurs to me that I really don't know the difference between the term homosexuality and lesbian. Does homosexuality cover it all, or does it only apply to a man?

August 27 from Crystal

Homosexuality means same-sexuality. It covers all same-sex love. Lesbian is a term somehow taken from the Greek island of Lesbos (don't ask me how), and applied to gay girls. However, gay and homo still refer to all gays. Faggot is just for guys, lesbian is just for girls

August 28 from Janet Arthur

Re the Bible: I have been taught that the Bible is inspiration and revelation. Also, I believe that I have read that the NT is the explanation of the OT or perhaps the fulfillment of the OT—it is a completion of the story. Jesus was sent from God to personally take on everyone's sins, whatever they might be. And it is through Jesus that we find God.

The OT pretty much teaches "Be good or be punished." But the NT deals more with love: "For God so loved the world that he sent his only begotten Son," (John 3:16) I believe that there is also a story of a man who is in hell calling up to Jesus to save him and take him into Paradise, and Jesus refuses. The man then says," At least let a drop of water fall into my mouth," and Jesus refuses. Then the man says, "At least let me appear to my brothers and tell them that eternal punishment is real," and Jesus refuses, saying, "They have the same chances that you had to believe." (Luke 16:19-31)

That God loves us is real—that we are given all the necessary time to believe is real, but so is eternal punishment if we choose to turn away from God.

I'll tell you one thing though—you made me look up my Bible! It was downstairs.

By the way, you mentioned the Isle of Lesbos and I looked it up on-line. According to Wikipedia I found that there was a once a famous female Greek poet by the name of Sappho who wrote of romantic love between women. Because she had a school on the island, she is sometimes called the "first lesbian".

Also, FYI, a "faggot" is a bundle of sticks tied together and was used to burn people at the stake during the Spanish Inquisition.

P.S. If you don't want me to ask personal questions about your beliefs or sexual orientation, just tell me so.

Luv,
G'ma

August 29 from Crystal

But then, how do you respond to Christians who say that the bible is infallible, as it is written by god? They treat it as a history book.

Now, you're gonna have to explain this whole sin thing to me ... Because the way it looks is this: God is angry and violent and strict. If you do something he doesn't want you to do, he'll kill your whole village. Then he suddenly decides to make himself human so that he can be killed brutally by humans. Is that something of an apology from god? But he can't apologize, because he is infallible, right?! But then he'll still make you endure eternal pain if you don't believe in him … What kind of a loving god is that? Can't he love without requiring constant worship and praise in return? Sounds like a tyrant to me.

On the subject of bibles … four years ago, while I was in the process of growing out of my Christian beliefs, I opened up a bible to a random page …

Do you know the story of Lot? (Genesis 19:1–38) Four men came to his house, and he thought they must be angels. Then people from his town came by and told him to give them the men, because they wanted them for sex. Lot argued with them. Then he offered them his virgin daughters instead. Apparently, that was the right thing to do. It is quite the shocking story.

Anyway, on a lighter note, college is going okay. I had to spend $622 on books just for three classes, though.

—Crystal

August 30 from Crystal

Actually, I've happened into a sort of discussion about the OT vs. the NT with one of my new college friends. He says it's supposed to be metaphorical, basically.

Oh, but why did god feel he had to hurt himself in order to pay himself for our "sins"?

And wow, that's a really sick story about the guy in hell. No one deserves to burn for eternity. Why would you believe that someone does? It can only make them into worse people than they already are. Why not just destroy them? After all, God doesn't seem to follow the laws of science, right? So the laws of thermodynamics don't apply to him. So he could destroy matter if he wanted to. So why not do that? If god so loves, why would he condemn someone to eternal suffering? Why not just get rid of them permanently? What's the point?

—-Crystal

P.S. Go ahead and ask about my beliefs and sexual orientation.

P.S.S. But wait a minute ... You already asked about my beliefs; so now you're asking about my sexual orientation?

September

I felt that I was over my head with answering her on the Old Testament, so I sent a message to "Ask-A-Franciscan," asking the Catholic support network of Franciscan priests to help me formulate a response to my granddaughter. Then I forwarded that exchange to Crystal.

September 17 forwarded from Janet Arthur

Dear Janet Arthur,
Your Ask-A-Franciscan question has been answered (with a lot of bold capitalization which I left out.).

Question:

My 18-year-old granddaughter now proclaims herself atheist because of the way that the church treats homosexuals and because of the Old Testament and the cruel judgments that God makes. For example: The story of Lot and his giving of his daughters to be raped.

Answer:

The answer was long and often in caps but in essence said that: God loves all human beings. He wants everyone to be treated with respect. The Catholic Church admonishes us to encourage everyone to understand their sexuality, and appreciate the power of sexuality. Finally, the letter goes on to say that anger is a human attribute of God; however, in the light of the New Testament, it is Jesus that shows us by His life and sacrifice that God is always moving us to unity and peace. Jesus gave His life for us that "we might have life, and have life in abundance: John10:10

The letter ends with: Thank you for visiting Ask-A-Franciscan. Peace and all good!

September 19 from Crystal

Wow. What was up with all the capitalization? Was it written by a thirteen-year-old?

And actually, that is not why I'm an atheist. I started questioning my Christian beliefs when I saw the way the church and the religious right treated homosexuals. One question led to another, and I eventually realized that there's no such thing as god.

That's a really good blog, by the way.

September 23 from Janet Arthur

Hey—I'm waiting here for some controversial thoughts—or at least, a Hi, how are you?

I did hear one question: Would you rather be a happy, fulfilled pig or an unhappy, unfulfilled philosopher? (John Stewart Mill)[5]

G'ma

---

5 John Stewart Mill, *Utilitarianism,* chapter 2. The full quote is "It is better to be a human being dissatisfied than a pig satisfied; better to be Socrates than a fool satisfied. And if the fools, or the pig, are of different opinion, it is because they only know their own side of the question."

September 24 from Crystal

Hmmm … Philosopher, 'cause then I'd feel smart!!! But at the same time … hmmm … well, it's like saying ignorance is bliss. Would you rather be blissful or unhappy? I dunno.

By the way: This morning I broke up with Trey. Just this morning, and it didn't go the way I'd planned. Trey's mom loves me because I made Trey better than he was. But it's really no consolation.

I am happy to be single, though. I plan on staying that way for at least a month or two … And then just see what happens.

Am I being selfish?

Did I do the right thing?

September 28 from Crystal

Hi, Grandma!!

How did the surgery go? Mom said everyone has been taking care of you. What's kept you away from your computer?

I felt like giving you an update on my social life, though, because I've been drowning in my own drama, which has … not happened many times before.

So, anyway, this is what has been going on with me:

Ann Marie, (allegedly straight) decided it'd be a fun idea to make out with me. Trey desperately wants me back; Pat from work asked me out; John from work likes me; Robert P. from school may or may not like me, and Jessica from school has mentioned having dibs on me or something …

Also, I've been having a lot of trouble concentrating on homework and on my classes, though I'm still passing my classes with *A*s.

I AM attracted to John, but … I couldn't see myself dating him. He's more masculine than what I would normally go after, so it'd be weird. He intimidates me in that way. Also, he hangs out with a different group of people in the group at K-Building than I do. I don't mesh with his group of friends, and that would be NOT GOOD.

Now about Robert: The one thing I didn't like about him is that he's a Christian, but I've actually gotten over that now. Ha, this is what college is all about! Expanding your horizons! Still, I think my chances with him are slim. He says he's not ready for another relationship.

Of course, neither am I—I'm definitely waiting a month before dating anyone. I was originally hoping to keep my mind off dating altogether, but it seems that that is impossible.

Er … I don't know what else to say about him—he's awesome. But, morally speaking, I really shouldn't pursue him at all. I did break the hearts of the last *2* people I dated. Still, if I was given the opportunity to date him, I don't think I'd be able to say no. Then again, I don't really know what he'd be like in a relationship, what with the whole touching thing. He told me the first time a girl hugged him, he got all shaky. He's afraid of firsts. I'm the first person he's cuddled with … He told me afterwards that he was happy and terrified at the same time. Now I don't know what to think.

Basically, I am having lots and lots of social drama. Gee, and I was so comfy dealing with my friends' drama from the sidelines!! Bleh.

But other than all of that, things are going well for me. I have a great job, I've made friends, and I'm doing well in school.

Advice, please?

—Crystal

October

I feel that I dropped the ball here because of not replying sooner. I had knee surgery and was unable to sit at my computer Also; I think that my pain pills got me to wax a bit too eloquent when I did respond.

However, Crystal, who was friendless in high school, seems to have finally blossomed into many friendships, and I keep warning her to go slow.

October 7 from Janet Arthur

Hi—sorry it has taken me so long to reply—the reason being: pain and exercise. I'm almost 3 weeks post-op now and starting to sleep and be crabby—a sure sign of recovery!

I did however, read your "Social Drama" e-mail, and this is my response:

Dearest Crystal—Did I never tell you that we are descendants of Irish Royalty? Our ancestral home is Castle Caldwell in Ireland. Of course people are attracted to us—our proud bearing, dignity, deportment, charisma, intelligence—we see all and disdain many. We go our own way and carve new paths—and our fast mouths often get us into trouble. 'Tis a terrible burden to be so gifted—many are called but few are chosen …

I do have to warn you though of our natural tendency to feel that we are so strong that we can nurture the weak. Sometimes we fear the strength we feel in others and feel more secure with the lesser person. Wrong! The person you are looking for is equally as strong and attractive as you—don't fear him—see him as an equal. If you want to take care of someone—be a doctor!

Hold yourself safe and valuable—be kind when you can, and keep up the good grades in school.

Proud of you!

Love,

G'ma

October 8 from Crystal

I'm glad you've recovered enough to get to your email! I've been anxious for a reply.

I'm kind of weirded out by this email you sent, though. (Were you on anything when you typed it? It's filled with spelling errors and vague advice …)

But I, for the first time, get where you're coming from with that whole "if you want to take care of someone, then be a doctor" (something I always say) thing. I do feel more secure with lesser persons. I've actually noticed that I have this problem. I have a desire to help and I do feel that I am strong enough to nurture the weak.

This is one of the reasons I'm so stoked to have Robert for a friend. I haven't actually been friends with someone who's on par with me intellectually before. (Well, actually, he's probably a bit smarter than me.) It's great! But I'm also incredibly attracted to him ... But I value him as a friend before anything else. I've decided to pursue him, but very, very, cautiously. I know this time I need to make sure me and my potential lovers are on the same page when it comes to intentions and expectations. There would have to be a talk before anything emotionally serious stuff happened.

I am assuming he's interested, of course. It is true that he's rejected many, many girls over the past few years. But, then again, no other girl has gotten this close, so ... I think I've got a shot? I mean, he's visited me at work almost every day I've been scheduled for the past couple weeks, plus there's the whole cuddling thing. Of course, we both loudly claim to anyone who inquires that the cuddling is merely platonic and has resulted in casual intimacy. Sometimes we both just need a hug.

School and work continue to go well, and my social life is enjoyable. I hope all is well with you also.

—Crystal

P.S. Robert has been debating me while you were "away."

October 9 from Janet Arthur

Hi—sorry about the typos and the Irish thing—though it is true that, on my side, we are descendants of Irish Kings. I wanted you to be proud of yourself and to look around at our family and see that we are smart and do attract attention and do have to be careful of "lesser" types. You have so much to look forward to, now the world is your oyster—pick a pearl!

But "lover"—why do we immediately go there? Enjoy the thrill of just being with Robert, and do it with restraint. Be careful of letting anyone into the "core" Crystal.

Great to be back!

Luv, G'ma

October 10 from Janet Arthur

Hey—I love that you are having more introspective thoughts about your choices of boy friends. Way to Go!

As for me, I could actually get my socks on by myself today and even do a little cleaning—not that I love cleaning—but I love feeling that I can.

Going for a drive to Aunt Barbara's tomorrow—it will be my first outing, and I'm excited.

Love hearing from you—I'm living vicariously through you—how's that for a thought!

Luv,

October 11 from Crystal

So that sucks. What have you been doing in your spare time, while so restricted?

You're living vicariously through me? Ah, so you don't mind hearing me blabber on about Robert and such? Huzzah!

So, the first kiss went very well. The next day, when we went to a haunted hayride with his family, I kissed him in the backseat of the car on the way home.

I also kissed him a few times on the hayride, but on the cheek. It was funny, because his sister Jessica's boyfriend was like "aww" and Jessica was all upset because she missed it. "Do it again! I missed it!"

T'was funny because they were so excited, but I like his sister and her boyfriend (even though he's straight edge).

But yeah, I did end up going too fast for him, though. He came over to my house afterwards, and we were making out on my couch. He was trembling during most of it. It was one of those "terrified and happy at the same time" things.

But then, yesterday, he came over to my house after I got off of work, and he was fine. Interestingly, he and I have the same kissing style. Also, he's the first person I've really enjoyed kissing with. His kisses are tentative and gentle. I love it. I've never really liked kissing all too much, especially when it comes to using tongue, but kissing him is exciting and wonderful.

Anyway, I gotta go to work. Write back!

October14 from Janet Arthur
Sounds like you may be going a little fast with Robert. Don't let him go where his emotions get away from him—remember he is his mom's boy too. Be as respectful of him as I want him to be of you. Don't spoil something that could be very sweet.

With all this romance going on—how is school? How are your grades on papers, tests? Remember Prime Time goes to school—the rest is frosting. Enjoy!!

Luv,
G'ma

October 15 from Crystal
AHA! I KNEW you were drugged! Hahaha, I feel perceptive!

Yes, the first day was a bit too much for him overall. But after that day, he's been fine. And don't worry; I do respect his boundaries and all that.

As for school, let's see …

My English teacher doesn't give a grade higher than 96% on an essay. But she also will not give anyone a zero on anything. I end up sleeping through English a lot, just because it's so ridiculous. The other day, she explained to us what nouns and verbs are. I hate it. But I guess I enjoy the break.

Math is going okay now that I'm in the right class.

Industrial/Organizational Psychology is, of course, my favorite class. It's not the most interesting psychology subject, but it's my most interesting class at the moment.

My bodybuilding class starts up next week.

As for work, it's going just fine. I deposit all of my paychecks, and I use my tips for weekly needs (such as food).

I'm going to be going shopping for clothes next weekend with Mom, so I'm pretty excited about that. I only have a few pairs of guy pants, and I really need some more. I haven't carried a purse in forever, and I don't want to start again.

—Crystal

October 16 from Janet Arthur

Hi—so you went around telling everyone that your grandmother was on drugs, eh? I defy you to do this knee thing without them!

You are taking a bodybuilding class—that should be interesting.

I'm pretty impressed with your saving program—it's great!

English: remember, the teacher owns the room; you just have to get the highest grade that you can. Sometimes it's not fair. My sister would have graduated magna cum laude, but her English teacher (high school) said that he hadn't assigned any "A" work.

So try to look interested; she is trying to include the whole class—even those who may not know what verbs and nouns are.

Try to have a good time shopping with your mother. I went shopping with Aunt Sarah once, and we started with her telling me she was too tall and me saying, "Who told you that?" It went downhill from there. Try to be understanding and happy with your mom; she wants to give you a good memory.

Luv,

From your ditzy G'ma

October 17 from Crystal

Aw, I don't blame you for using drugs! I would too, of course.

Yes, shopping with my mom has never been a pleasant occasion. I will try to make it so this time, though.

As for that English teacher, you've got her wrong. I neglected to explain the full incompetence of this woman. She's extremely lazy. For one thing, she doesn't even have her own syllabus. She's following the syllabus of another teacher. Her notes are taken directly from the textbook. Plus, the other day, she was complaining to us that one of her students wrote an 8-page essay. The assignment was

2–3 pages. She complained because it took her so long to read.

Believe me; she is not simply trying to include the whole class. She's just up there at the front of the classroom, repeating the words from our textbook, chapter by chapter. She can't even manage to fill up the entire hour and a half of class time. We always get out 15 or 30 minutes early. It's really quite pathetic. My friend Tara is particularly upset about the situation, because she loves English, and she is going to college to learn. As for me, as I've probably already told you, I couldn't care less about this class. After witnessing this teacher's incompetent performance on the first day of class, I spoke to her straight away to find out what grade I could expect to get out of her.

She told me most of the people in her Composition II class aced it. And so, I am quite content with the situation.

Crystal

P.S. I am sending a political cartoon video

October 30 from Janet Arthur
[*Crystal sent me a music video of Obama and McCain rhyming and harmonizing, "Vote for me." It was pretty funny.*]

Hi. I thought the video was very well done and the graphics and image look-a-likes were very good. Making fun of politics seems to be about all we can do at this point

What are you doing for Halloween?—It is supposed to be nice out—Do you and Robert have plans? We are looking forward to meeting him; he sounds nice.

Keep in touch
Luv,

October 30 from Crystal

Yes, the video was very cool. John showed it to me.

I don't agree that making fun of them is all we can do at this point. Of course, I feel quite strongly about my choice for president.

—Crystal

October 31 from Crystal

There is a song called "The Great Debate," by Dream Theater, which presents both sides of the Stem Cell Research Controversy. I was recently turned on to this song, so I thought I'd send it to you, considering all of the controversy. The song does not take a side, but argues both sides of the issue. It's a really good song. I'm in love with it.

Oh, by the way, Rachel, at work, got fired, because John caught her in the back room having sex with her boyfriend.

But anyway, now that she is gone I get to work every other Thursday in addition to my other hours, so I'm happy about that.

Anyway, gotta go!

—Crystal

November

Now that Crystal is working, she is having more real-life experiences. I think that the manager, John, is looking out for Crystal, and I hope that Crystal sees the immediate consequence of immoral behavior.

November 3 from Janet Arthur

Hi—isn't life interesting? And it just about always comes back to bite you. Just when you think nobody knows your secret, somebody is watching. How do I know all that you say? By living a long life and observing the happenings around me.

I always wonder how anybody thinks that they can get away with murder—or theft—someone always sees "something" out of the ordinary and investigates. (I watch a lot of TV.) And the thing is that the deed was never worth the price that is paid. They could have just divorced, etc. The moral to the story is to work hard and (I was going to say keep your "nose clean", but it sounded rather vile) ... you get the picture. Never do anything that you can't defend or are morally ashamed of. Even if not found out, you know, and you carry it like "Morley's chains," unless of course you go to confession, which is a very healthy psychological exercise.

Anyway, should go do exercises.

As always, I love hearing from you!

Luv,

G'ma

November 4 from Crystal

Would you like to elaborate on all of this? You send me this advice out of the blue. Obviously, there's a life story to go with it! I'd like to hear it.

I do know that you shouldn't do anything morally unsound for just those reasons that you laid out. But I will keep a focus on that, for now. Don't worry; I'm not doing anything that I wouldn't be able to defend. I am a moral person—you know that—and I'm not doing anything illegal, either. Really, I haven't even been presented with a chance to do anything illegal, like drinking.

—Crystal

November 5 from Janet Arthur

Hi—

Re: 10/31 e-mail: Sorry, thought I was obvious—"Rachael snuck a boy into a room for sex and got caught." Why would John "happen" to come in at that time? Because he had a feeling something was not right, and he decided to check and see what she was doing in the back room.

Luv,

G'ma

December

It was so good to get together with the whole family at Christmas. We were all excited to meet Robert, Crystal's new boyfriend. However, Crystal and her cousin Tina, who were once so close, now seemed to be very distant. Tina came alone, so that may have sparked some competition that I was unaware of. I just saw them avoiding each other.

When they were both very young, we took them to our cottage—we have a great video of them. In it, Crystal says, "I saw a rainbow today, and I'm going to take it home with me.

Tina says, "You can't take it home, because rainbows belong to everybody"!

I loved those times.

December 27 from Crystal

When you asked me, at Mom's birthday party, why Tina and I no longer get along, I told you it was because we are different people. It isn't really a pleasant subject, and

I didn't want to have a discussion like that on my mom's birthday.

It is true that we don't get along anymore because of our differences; however, the main reason (as I see it, anyway) is that she has always looked down on me, and continues to do so. I don't blame her. I know how I used to be. I know I used to act out. I know I didn't mature as quickly as she did.

As things are right now, I have changed quite a bit in the past half a year from moving here and going to college, and I had even grown up a lot in the year preceding that.

But she's always going to see me the way she's always known me to be. After all, we only see each other once or twice a year. This became particularly obvious at your Christmas dinner when Tina said she could definitely believe that I was being immature.

It used to bother me a lot, but after that experience, I sorted out my feelings and came to the conclusion that I've just shared with you. And, really, her feelings or attitudes about me don't matter to me any more. I understand her position; I understand that I am not the person she sees when she looks at me, and I understand that her views are not going to change, and they don't have to affect me at all. I only see her a couple times a year, so she doesn't make any sort of difference in my life, or my perception of myself.

So, there it is. That is the reason why she and I haven't been best buds since we were in elementary school and the reason why we're not very friendly with each other now.

Crystal

January

Christmas is past, and we got to meet Robert, who was tall, good looking, and courteous. He told me right at the door that he was really shy. We saw him as smart, very nice, and polite. But since Rick was there, Crystal didn't even want Robert to speak to him and that did cause some awkwardness, especially since her cousin Tina was there.

January 25 from Janet Arthur
Aww—Prickly Pear, that makes me feel sad. I loved it when you two were my "Rose White" and "Rose Red" (Crystal is pale with blond hair; her cousin is dark haired and always looks tanned). Of course, you are different— that's what makes it interesting. Yes, she got interested in boys before you did, but that's just a minor glitch in life. It is like the new camera that can take many pictures of the same thing and link them together by attaching them at their similarities. They did it on CNN with all the pictures people sent in of the inauguration and could make one huge picture. You and Tina are part and parcel of this

family and come together at many places to make up our whole family; you're both just growing into yourselves. How could Tina look down on you? There was never anything wrong with you! You had to go through a little bit nastier patch of life than she did and, by the way, you were the one that got scholarships—and who was it who could barely make it into Western? Tina probably thinks that you look down on her!

You two are like the front and back of the same coin—Tina knows that she is pretty and doesn't know that she is smart. You, on the other hand, know that you are smart, but you don't know that you are pretty! What you both have forgotten is that you are gifts to each other and could be great buds through the coming years—don't close any doors that can lead you down a wonderful, rewarding path.

Luv,

G'ma

P.S. I don't remember anything said about you being immature at Christmas.

P.P.S. Keep writing—we are on our way down south, and I am at Aunt Julie's now. I didn't get a laptop, but I can check my mail at the hotel or library.

January 26 from Crystal

Gosh, I don't even know where to start.

She got interested in boys before I did? That's not what I meant when I said she matured sooner than I did. She did start wearing girly stuff and makeup before I did, and I only did that for about a year anyway, but actually, I was referring to the fact that I was still playing pretend until I turned ten. And I wasn't even playing normal pretend (let's play house!) I was pretending I was a dog or whatever.

Also, at some point during family gatherings, she started hanging out with the older cousins, while I was still hanging out with Megan, Timothy, etc. Soon enough, she stopped hanging out with us altogether. At family gatherings, you'll notice that she sits at the "adult table" and chitchats with the adults, while Timothy and I are off doing something else somewhere else. You know what I mean?

I agree that Tina and I are similar in various ways. But the reason why we don't get along is her *perception* of me because of our differences and our pasts, not because of the differences themselves.

She has plenty of reason to look down on me. I played pretend until the age of 10! Even the girls I went to school with made fun of me and called me immature. I was incredibly gullible as an elementary-school child (and she used that to her full advantage, which she has on occasion reminded me of. I don't remember any of it, though). I wasn't interested in girly anything. I acted out for attention.

She grew up very fast and became very feminine. I took my time, and did most of my emotional maturing during the past year and a half. And I never became at all feminine. I wore makeup for a year, after I went through puberty, and that was it.

She's a preppie, and I'm just one of the odd kids.

So, of course she looks down on me. And of course, she thinks I'm immature. I don't think she thinks I look down on her. But you can ask her about it if you like.

That's a cute coin analogy, but not true. I can't say whether or not Tina knows she's smart, but I sure as hell know I'm pretty. I know how attractive I am. I don't have to wear makeup or flashy clothes, because I am not worried about how I look—I know I'm attractive. I mean, if I were unattractive, I would probably be much more concerned about how I look. That's not to say that girls who care about that are really unattractive; I'm just saying that in my case, that's probably how it is.

Just because we're all close in age and related doesn't mean we should become friends. We only see each other once a year. Not that I discourage friendship from anyone. I don't. But it doesn't matter to me. If it matters to them, they could simply approach me and befriend me.

It did hurt that Tina looks down on me, but it doesn't anymore. I talked to John about it, and he helped me realize what I've been telling you. I can't change her perceptions of me; only she can. But it doesn't matter, because her perceptions of me cannot affect me unless I let them.

—Crystal

P.S. You wouldn't remember the incident at Christmas, because you weren't part of that conversation. The reason she called me immature was because I had asked Robert not to get friendly with Rick, because of my feelings toward Rick. Robert has a philosophy of neutrality, and we ended up fighting about it. I just didn't want to deal with Rick, hear his voice, and especially not see him getting friendly with my boyfriend. You know how Rick is. He just seems so very nice at the beginning, and he makes people like him.

I admit that I was being a bit unreasonable. But I still think that my request wasn't much to ask.

January 31 from Janet Arthur

Once again, prickly pear, you are making me feel bad. I believed in Santa Claus until I was at least ten—maybe twelve! As far as girl stuff—I like nice stuff. Girly, hmm, I always think that you are making some kind of statement by wearing baggy clothes. Not sure what that statement is.

But sometimes you do have to go through a phase, and then be the first one to open a door to friendship, just to let others know that you are ready for a new relationship.

As far as times of contact are concerned, I have a friend in Traverse City that I grew up with and only see once or every other year, and we start right where we left off.

Well, must go—time to leave for Hilton Head.

Love you,

G'ma

February

Here Crystal really reveals a lot about herself and how she sees herself. I didn't realize that she had been made fun of in grade school. However, once I did clothes-shop with her, and "girly stuff" did make her uncomfortable and itchy. However, I do think that Crystal may wish that she did fit into her more girlish cousin Tina's world.

February 6 from Crystal
Sorry about the whole prickly pear thing. I was just feeling emotional. I almost started crying in front of John at one point. It really gets to me when people call me immature, probably because that's how the other girls made fun of me when I was a kid. It also really gets to me when someone makes fun of me for being stupid. I guess I've still got low self-esteem.

I guess I took after you then, with the rate of maturity! ☺ As for the baggy clothes, I like comfortable clothes. As far back as I can remember (6 maybe?), I always abhorred anything girly. I've no idea why, but I did. "Sissy" was a mean insult, and pink was an ugly color. That dislike has certainly carried over all the way to my present.

But I only started shopping in the boys' section when I was fifteen. Before it occurred to me to do that, I shopped in the girls' section, where it was very difficult to find clothing that I liked. Most female clothing is made to look good, not to feel good. The shirts are too thin. They're too short (if I raise my hand, my shirt lifts, exposing my belly). Ruffles itch. The pants ride too low (if I squat or bend over, the pants move, exposing my butt-crack).

It was so difficult to find plain, comfortable clothing. (Oddly enough, Timothy and I have opposite opinions about this. He thinks that girl's clothing is more comfortable, and that's what he likes to wear.) Boy's clothing is made for its function. That's why I wear it.

I have been buying tighter shirts, though. I look like I'm fourteen, so I am attempting to look older by accentuating my boobs.

As for the baggy pants, I wear those because I do not carry a purse, and I need somewhere to keep my phone, money, and ID. Girl pants don't typically have big enough pockets for my needs. I don't carry a purse for the same reason I don't wear jewelry. It would only get in the way. I'm not gonna leave my purse lying around, so that means I have to carry it. Meaning it'll get in the way; it'll be a nuisance. I would actually like to wear jewelry every once in a while, since it can look very cool, but once again, it gets in the way. I used to wear a watch, which I was becoming accustomed to wearing because it was useful—I used it all the time.

So, basically, I'm a big, whiny baby that can't stand to wear anything that doesn't feel good or serve a purpose. I do have an aversion to feminine stuff, though.

I know that you have to be the first to offer the hand of friendship, in most cases. But I think the distance is a good thing, for now. Maybe someday, when we're older, Tina and I will reconnect.

Crystal

March

I am on vacation now, and so correspondence has been spotty. But Emily sent me a phone picture of Crystal with her beautiful hair all cut off. I think it looks terrible and wonder if it is a further sign that she is questioning of her sexuality. On the other hand when I was in high school I bleached my hair, just my bangs, blond. I still remember my dad saying to my mom, "Mary, did you see what she did to herself? I guess maybe I was "acting out"!

March 1 from Janet Arthur
Hey you—

Your mother just sent me a photo of you with your beautiful hair cut off! Please send me a note telling me about it

Be home soon

Love,

G'ma

March 2 from Crystal

I took Timothy to get his hair cut on Sunday, and I decided I wanted mine cut the same way. I've always thought about cutting my hair really short, but I've never had the courage to do it before. *(What if it doesn't look good? What if I have to style it every day? It'll be a pain in the ass to grow back out again!)* I dunno; I've made two best friends, and I'm feeling rather confident right now. I figure if I'm ever going to experiment with my hair, now is the time to do it. I'm a college student now, so I can. (Plus, I'm not job-searching and won't be for quite some time) And I'm such a rebel; I asked my boss if it was okay first! Ha ha ha (she laughed at me for asking.)

Anyway, overall, I'm pretty happy with it. All I have to do to style it in the morning is get it soaking wet and then let it dry (I wake up with horrible bed hair now). I can straighten it if I want, but I don't have to. Also, the hair looks awesome under a hat. Jessie and Samantha say I look like a flapper girl now.

The one thing I don't like about it is that I've been told it makes me look younger. But as much as I want to look my age, I know that's never going to happen, and the haircut's pros outweigh the cons.

Did you also hear that Robert and I broke up? ☹

April

Cutting hair for a female can be quite an emotional time, as is breaking up with a boyfriend, so I am worried about Crystal. And yet, her mother doesn't seem to be concerned.

April 4 from Janet Arthur
Hi—

Sorry about Robert—we really liked him.

Re: The hair—from the picture, I can't say that I like it, but the picture is on a camera phone, and so I think distorted. Your mom is just delighted that you are delighted! I think that I need to see you to have an opinion. You have such beautiful hair. My experience is: I took my long, beautiful hair for granted and the first time that I cut it, Grandpa asked me not to, and I said, "Why not? It's just hair!" The end of the story is that I never had the time to get that long hair again, and now I'm sorry, and my hair was never as nice again—plus you get too old to have your hair long. Sometimes I think of riding on the bus with the window open and the breeze just lifting my hair off my shoulders. Umm.

G'ma

P.S. It is good to be able to correspond again.

P.P.S. Was your hair cut at a beauty shop?

Luv, G'ma

April 6 from Crystal

Yeah, I liked him as well. Still do, actually … We have the same group of friends, so we're still friends with each other.

I'm happy to have dated him. I got exactly what I wanted out of the relationship, and more. It hurts that it's over, but it was for the best. We both knew that is only a short-term relationship; we weren't a good match, and he's certainly not the type of person I'm looking for to settle down with (no religion allowed). And I'm nowhere near ready to settle down yet.

The haircut was at a beauty shop.

Crystal

June

In April, just as soon as we got home from our vacation, I had my second knee surgery. Knee surgery is painful at first, and you must elevate your legs and keep them iced, and so that is what I did in May. Finally, I am able to sit up at my computer again to re-read our e-mails and continue to write to Crystal.

June 10 from Janet Arthur
Hi—you and I haven't talked for a while

I was just reading over our e-mails and got to the one where you say all stupid people should be sterilized. Do you still believe that? It's very Nazi you know—Hitler felt the same way about anyone that was Catholic or Jewish—or had something that he wanted—they were deformed, to his way of thinking, and so he could excuse their elimination.

Also, Re: Wiccan belief about not harming anyone—how does that fit with abortion? You said that you loved their beliefs.

I heard that you and Robert had been dating again and then broke up again—can you still be friends with him now? How is life in general? What are you doing this summer?

Miss you.

Luv,

G'ma

July

Because of the time lapse, I feel that we have lost some of the closeness and intimacy of our earlier e-mails. I now hesitate to prod too much. I don't know if I can regain her trust.

The good thing now is that in my absence, Crystal has become closer to her mother, and I am glad. However, I miss the specialness of hearing her thoughts.

July 10 from Crystal
Ha, yeah, I remember that. No, of course I didn't really mean it. I do understand that intelligence is based more on environment than genetics. Intelligence levels are pretty much the same from country to country. What we need is not sterilization, but programs to give kids an opportunity to grow, mentally.

I just get kind of bitter sometimes because there are some REALLY stupid people out there, and it seems like they're the ones spawning the most children. (And, of course, stupid people tend to raise stupid children.) They're a menace! I do think there needs to be a cap on the number of kids we're allowed to have. Think of the woman with eighteen kids. What's that show called … *Seventeen and Counting,* and she home-schools all of them. She doesn't have the time or the education to teach that many children. She's not even teaching them any science.

The Wiccan belief is very close to the Golden Rule. Do unto others what you would have them do unto you. That's the only rule you need. When making a moral decision, you just need to think to yourself, "What would the world be like if everyone did this?" And that should give you a huge hint as to whether or not you're doing the right thing. How does that fit into abortion? Well, the Wiccan's say "An' it harm none, do as you will." By having an abortion, not only are you not harming anyone, you're saving yourself (and the unborn child as well) a lot of hardship.

Yes, I broke up with Robert about a month ago. We *are* still friends, though not the same as we were before. Robert has changed somewhat, and I'm not really comfortable with that change. But we do have the same group of friends, and it is important that we get along. We get along really well at the moment.

Life in general is okay. I've had a really hectic summer. I've encountered an astounding number of problems, and only a few of them are mine—how I look … I'm highly unlikely to make a comment about how hot I am. I know I'm attractive. Hell, I have seven people crushing on me RIGHT NOW. But it's never been super important to me. It's never consumed all of my thoughts. You should be able to tell that I'm not concerned with how attractive I am to others just by looking at me.

This summer I plan on having as much fun as possible, and spending as much time with friends as I can! I've acquired quite a few friends since last year, so I don't ever have to spend an evening bored at home. I've also acquired two best friends, and I spend most of my time with them. We go to the gym together three nights a week and we're planning on taking over the Gay–Straight Alliance at our school together in the fall.

—Crystal

G'ma's Note

And so I feel that this is a good a place to end. It's been a year of growing and learning. Crystal has turned from a silent, sulking teen to a self-starting young woman with a lot of friends. She certainly has developed a lot of opinions, and though I don't agree with most of them, I do admire her individuality and her spunk. And I hope that if she at last chooses a "person" for her life that it will be one that has the qualities of Robert.

My daughter did know about the e-mails and encouraged me to help Crystal vent. Now, as I re-read them, I feel that they might be relevant and offer some helpful insights to other families going through the similar circumstances: divorce, remarriage, difficulty with stepparents and stepchildren, religious defiance, and teen rebellion. I also feel that they show the interesting workings of the teenage mind vs. the more mature mind.

I took a seminar once called "What You Are Is Where You Were When." It spoke of how differently you see the world depending on how the world looked to you at the age of ten. To Crystal, I now realize, the world is indeed different from the one that I remember and continue to feel to be right.

I now feel that all generations should listen to each other with compassion and open hearts and minds to each other. Obviously, we both disclose what many would call the "flaws" in our own belief systems. These are our—mostly on my part—unsupported opinions, garnered from years of living in this sometimes confusing world.

As our lives continue to develop, I hope the communication with my granddaughter continues. I just spent the day with Crystal and she hopes so too. That is all the hope anyone can ask for.

Crystal's Note

These emails document the first time I ever put my thoughts and feelings about the world into words and onto paper. It was the first time I'd ever explained them to anyone else: much less to someone who had an opposing viewpoint. I really enjoyed doing it. Not only did I learn how to argue better, I also formed a close relationship with my grandmother in the process. We often have opposing views, and we both enjoyed arguing them out with each other. However, now that it's all over and all of those emails are being published, I feel a little embarrassed about some of the things I've written.

Some of what I wrote was purposely inflammatory. I used to get a kick out of saying things that I thought might shock someone else, and in the case of these emails in particular; I often said things with the intention of starting a fight. Having arguments was the point of our emails, but it still embarrasses me a little bit to reread some of the stuff I said, which I would be much less likely to say today.

I've certainly cooled down a bit since then. I'm now an independent adult. No one is forcing me to go to church or say grace at dinner. I don't have to hide my sexual orientation. No one is financially responsible for me. In summary, I now have control over all aspects of my life. It took me over a year after moving out to do it, but I've lost most of that bitterness that all teenagers feel, some more intensely than others, at being forced to do things that they believe is wrong or just plain don't want to do. In addition to that, I have my worldview figured out, for the most part. I no longer feel the need to make inflammatory comments, because I don't need to have lots of arguments, and I don't seek to offend others.

In addition to making inflammatory statements, I also made wrong statements. There are some things that I said in those emails that I've since learned are untrue. I feel I must apologize to the reader. I was and still am ignorant about a lot of things. I'm now deeply immersed in LGBT—lesbian, gay, bisexual, and transgendered—culture, and I have confidence in my ability to argue about or speak on LGBT issues, but I'm not an expert on everything. When I wrote the emails, I was even less educated than I am now, including about LGBT issues. However, at the time, I felt perfectly confident in arguing about anything and everything, especially since I thought the only person who would ever read it would be my grandma. I only occasionally checked my facts, and I didn't do much research. I was not qualified to speak on a lot of the things I spoke about. I am mortified to think about all of the uneducated, ignorant things I may have written in those emails. I have not and don't plan on rereading all of them.

I've also softened on a few things, and changed my mind about a few others. I'm not as radical as I used to be. Again, I must attribute this change to the loss of my bitter, *angsty* teenaged outlook, which certainly fueled my more extreme and angry views.

You're probably wondering to yourself, "If she's so embarrassed by those emails, why did she agree to have them published?!" You're probably also hoping I'll list examples of some of the stuff I referenced above, but I'm afraid I must disappoint you there. I'd really rather not dwell on those things; no, not even to correct them. Anyway, the first reason why I gave her permission to publish them was because I didn't think she'd actually do it and so I didn't think too hard about whether or not I wanted them out there for the world to see. But as long as I'm under a pseudonym and no one ever connects me with this book, I don't see why it shouldn't be published. I agree with my grandmother that some people might find those emails an interesting read, so why should I stop them from reading it?

Would it be vain of me to assume you would like to know who I am and what I'm doing with my life now, about a year after the last email in the book? Well, I suppose if you read this far, you must be interested.

I am an active member of the LGBT community. My best friends and I run a Gay-Straight Alliance. We're also on a committee to create a Safe Zone Initiative, which has the goal of making our college campus a safer, more educated, and more accepting place of LGBT people through the creation of safe zones and trained LGBT allies.

I don't know if I was calling myself a feminist when I wrote those emails, or even if I knew what the word meant, but I now consider myself an active feminist. I occasionally make donations to Planned Parenthood, and I try to challenge sexism wherever I see it. I would really like to get more involved in the feminist movement, but the LGBT movement is where I'm putting that energy right now.

I am an atheist, though not an active one. There aren't really any opportunities for me to get involved in the atheist community, socially or politically. I stay connected to the atheist community by reading atheist blogs and the occasional book, but that's about it. I don't have debates about religion anymore. I try to be more sensitive to the feelings of religious people around me, but I'm still very much a "militant atheist." No one's forcing me to go to church anymore, but religion still has way too much power over my life. Thanks to the religious, conservative right, I can't marry a woman or serve in the military as an open bisexual. My right to control what happens to my body and choose whether or not I want to be pregnant is under attack. There are still times in my life when I feel just as bitter about religion, Christianity in particular, as I did when I was in high school.

I am still childless by choice and don't see any reason why I would change my mind about that.

I still don't know what career I want to pursue, and I am still majoring in psychology.

I just reread the epilogue that my grandma wrote, and I'm feeling a little self-centered. Her afterword and mine are both all about me! Now I guess I'd better write something about her—and avoid responding to her afterword with an argument.

I've always really admired my grandmother. The emails we sent back and forth just made me respect her all the more. Even though we have not arrived at the same conclusions, I know that she's a very intelligent woman, and her intelligence clearly shines through in her emails. Despite her age, she's still vibrant and on top of things, and I aspire to be the same way when I'm older. She's always challenging her mind in some way. As I write this, she is working on the project that is this book. Before this, I know she used to take art classes. She reads. She travels. She's pretty much amazing.

—Crystal Dent